VERY SHORT INTRODUCTIONS are for anyone wanting a stimulating and accessible way in to a new subject. They are written by experts and have been translated into more than 40 different languages. The series began in 1995 and now covers a wide variety of topics in every discipline. The VSI library contains nearly 400 volumes—a Very Short Introduction to everything from Indian philosophy to psychology and American history—and continues to grow in every subject area.

Very Short Introductions available now:

ACCOUNTING Christopher Nobes
ADVERTISING Winston Fletcher
AFRICAN HISTORY
    John Parker and Richard Rathbone
AGNOSTICISM Robin Le Poidevin
ALEXANDER THE GREAT Hugh Bowden
AMERICAN HISTORY Paul S. Boyer
AMERICAN IMMIGRATION David A. Gerber
AMERICAN POLITICAL PARTIES AND
    ELECTIONS L. Sandy Maisel
AMERICAN POLITICS Richard M. Valelly
THE AMERICAN PRESIDENCY
    Charles O. Jones
ANAESTHESIA Aidan O'Donnell
ANARCHISM Colin Ward
ANCIENT EGYPT Ian Shaw
ANCIENT GREECE Paul Cartledge
THE ANCIENT NEAR EAST Amanda H. Podany
ANCIENT PHILOSOPHY Julia Annas
ANCIENT WARFARE Harry Sidebottom
ANGELS David Albert Jones
ANGLICANISM Mark Chapman
THE ANGLO-SAXON AGE John Blair
THE ANIMAL KINGDOM Peter Holland
ANIMAL RIGHTS David DeGrazia
THE ANTARCTIC Klaus Dodds
ANTISEMITISM Steven Beller
ANXIETY Daniel Freeman and Jason Freeman
THE APOCRYPHAL GOSPELS Paul Foster
ARCHAEOLOGY Paul Bahn
ARCHITECTURE Andrew Ballantyne
ARISTOCRACY William Doyle
ARISTOTLE Jonathan Barnes
ART HISTORY Dana Arnold
ART THEORY Cynthia Freeland
ASTROBIOLOGY David C. Catling
ATHEISM Julian Baggini
AUGUSTINE Henry Chadwick
AUSTRALIA Kenneth Morgan
AUTISM Uta Frith
THE AVANT GARDE David Cottington
THE AZTECS David Carrasco

BACTERIA Sebastian G. B. Amyes
BARTHES Jonathan Culler
THE BEATS David Sterritt
BEAUTY Roger Scruton
BESTSELLERS John Sutherland
THE BIBLE John Riches
BIBLICAL ARCHAEOLOGY Eric H. Cline
BIOGRAPHY Hermione Lee
THE BLUES Elijah Wald
THE BOOK OF MORMON Terryl Givens
BORDERS Alexander C. Diener and Joshua Hagen
THE BRAIN Michael O'Shea
THE BRITISH CONSTITUTION
    Martin Loughlin
THE BRITISH EMPIRE Ashley Jackson
BRITISH POLITICS Anthony Wright
BUDDHA Michael Carrithers
BUDDHISM Damien Keown
BUDDHIST ETHICS Damien Keown
CANCER Nicholas James
CAPITALISM James Fulcher
CATHOLICISM Gerald O'Collins
CAUSATION
    Stephen Mumford and Rani Lill Anjum
THE CELL Terence Allen and Graham Cowling
THE CELTS Barry Cunliffe
CHAOS Leonard Smith
CHILDREN'S LITERATURE Kimberley Reynolds
CHINESE LITERATURE Sabina Knight
CHOICE THEORY Michael Allingham
CHRISTIAN ART Beth Williamson
CHRISTIAN ETHICS D. Stephen Long
CHRISTIANITY Linda Woodhead
CITIZENSHIP Richard Bellamy
CIVIL ENGINEERING David Muir Wood
CLASSICAL LITERATURE William Allan
CLASSICAL MYTHOLOGY Helen Morales
CLASSICS Mary Beard and John Henderson
CLAUSEWITZ Michael Howard
CLIMATE Mark Maslin
THE COLD WAR Robert McMahon
COLONIAL AMERICA Alan Taylor

Human Rights: A Very Short Introduction

Andrew Clapham

HUMAN RIGHTS

A Very Short Introduction

OXFORD
UNIVERSITY PRESS

OXFORD
UNIVERSITY PRESS

Great Clarendon Street, Oxford OX2 6DP

Oxford University Press is a department of the University of Oxford.
It furthers the University's objective of excellence in research, scholarship,
and education by publishing worldwide in

Oxford New York

Auckland Cape Town Dar es Salaam Hong Kong Karachi
Kuala Lumpur Madrid Melbourne Mexico City Nairobi
New Delhi Shanghai Taipei Toronto

With offices in

Argentina Austria Brazil Chile Czech Republic France Greece
Guatemala Hungary Italy Japan Poland Portugal Singapore
South Korea Switzerland Thailand Turkey Ukraine Vietnam

Oxford is a registered trade mark of Oxford University Press
in the UK and in certain other countries

Published in the United States
by Oxford University Press Inc., New York

British Library Cataloguing in Publication Data

Data available

Library of Congress Cataloging in Publication Data

Data available

ISBN 978-0-19-920552-3

12

Typeset by SPI Publisher Services, Pondicherry, India
Printed in Great Britain
by Ashford Colour Press Ltd., Gosport, Hampshire

Contents

Preface

The aim of this book is to provide the reader with some entry points into the worlds of human rights thinking, activism, and law. This book concentrates on the power of ideas to mobilize people against injustice and indignities. Human rights do not really resolve the tension between competing interests and various visions of how the world should be; rather, human rights ideas provide the vocabulary for arguing about which interests should prevail and how best to achieve the ends we have chosen.

This short introduction actually looks at the content of a number of rights rather than simply telling the human rights story of revolutions, proclamations, and continuing struggles. Calling for a world based on respect for human rights is easy; adjusting current arrangements to achieve full respect for human rights is a never-ending process when we consider that there are human rights to life, equality, free speech, privacy, health, food, and housing. Human rights are about each of us living in dignity, and we are a long way from achieving that on a global scale. We shall see that the human rights project is not simply about implementing a set of obligations fixed in history; rather, the human rights movement is about people standing up to injustice and showing solidarity in the face of oppression.

In order to allow readers to discover for themselves some of the texts and organizations referred to in this introduction, we have provided a website with internet links at http://hei.unige.ch/human-rights-vsi. References marked with an asterisk* in this book can be found on the website.

Acknowledgements

I should like to thank all those at Oxford University Press who worked to bring this project to fruition. Special thanks go to Marsha Filion, who saw through the initial ideas and lent her support at an important stage. I must also thank James Thompson, Alyson Silverwood and Zoe Spilberg for their hard work in the production of the book. In addition, I very much appreciated the constructive comments and encouragement I received from Susan Marks and the anonymous reviewers. Their enthusiasm, dedication, and suggestions certainly shaped the final product for the better. Thanks also go to Louise Petre for designing an elegant companion website for the book.

Here at the Graduate Institute of International Studies in Geneva, I have been fortunate to have access to assistance from excellent graduate students, who have posed pertinent questions and provided marvellous editorial help. I should like particularly to thank Michelle Healy and Claire Mahon for their help on this project.

Lastly, let me express my gratitude to two people from my family: my mother, Margaret Clapham, who nourished the project and read the manuscript with a critical eye to keeping it jargon-free,

and my wife, Mona Rishmawi, who not only offered unwavering
support, but also helped to shape the ideas and was happy to
'think aloud' with me on many occasions.

A.B.C.

Graduate Institute of International Studies,
Geneva

List of illustrations

Chapter 1
Looking at rights

These days it is usually not long before a problem is expressed as a human rights issue. This book looks at where the concept of human rights came from and how the human rights movement has developed a set of obligations that apply worldwide. We will consider the trajectory of the idea of human rights and the role that human rights play (and might come to play) in our world.

One theme of this introductory book is that different people currently see human rights in different ways. For some, invoking human rights is a heartfelt, morally justified demand to rectify all sorts of injustice; for others, it is no more than a slogan to be treated with suspicion, or even hostility. Lawyers sometimes consider that human rights represent almost a term of art, referring to the details of accepted national and international human rights law. Yet the application of human rights law is almost always contested, with both parties to a dispute demanding that human rights law be applied in their favour. Human rights law is special as it often suggests that other law is inadequate or unjust. The language of human rights is deployed to criticize, defend, and reform all sorts of behaviour. Playing the 'human rights card' can be persuasive, sometimes even conclusive, in contemporary decision making; this is one aspect of what makes the moral force of human rights so attractive – they help you to win arguments and, sometimes, to change the way things are done.

The concept of a 'human rights culture' also means different things to different people. To some, it means ensuring that everyone is treated with respect for their inherent dignity and human worth. To others, it means that judges, the police, and immigration officials are required to protect the interests of terrorists, criminals, and other undesirable elements at the expense of the security of the population. This tension recently came to a head in the United Kingdom with popular newspapers ridiculing the application of the new Human Rights Act (see Box 1). The tension is, in a way, inherent in the operation of human rights protections. Human rights come into play to stop governments and other actors from pursuing expedient policies at the expense of the well-being of certain individuals and the proper functioning of a democratic society under the rule of law. At times, human rights protections may seem to be anti-majoritarian; indeed, human rights may serve to protect people from the 'tyranny' of the majority. But, as we shall see, with the exception of the absolute ban on torture, human rights law does allow for security needs to be taken into consideration.

On closer inspection, much of the apparent British backlash against the 'human rights culture' in decision making turns out to be based on false information concerning the supposed effects of the new Human Rights Act. First, the judges cannot strike down laws as incompatible with human rights; Parliament retains complete sovereignty over which laws to pass or repeal. (This is not the case in other countries with an entrenched constitution, such as the United States or South Africa, where constitutional rights may rank supreme.) Second, the Government's review of the implementation of the Human Rights Act has highlighted a series of 'myths and misperceptions' about the Act. Stories, such as the prisoner who claimed that denial of access to certain magazines amounted to inhuman and degrading treatment, have been retold

2

Box 1: Human rights in the UK press

The Sun (online): Oliver Harvey and Michael Lea,* 'THOUSANDS of Sun readers have voted to scrap the Human Rights Act.'

Nearly 35,000 rang our You The Jury hotline within 24 hours to back our call for an end to the interests of killers, rapists and paedophiles coming ABOVE those of victims. The crazy legislation has led to many dangerous criminals being freed to re-offend. Others have used the barmy laws to gain perks and pay-outs.

The Sunday Telegraph: Give us back our rights

The Afghans who hijacked a civilian airliner are rewarded with a judgment that they are entitled to stay in Britain at the taxpayer's expense. Foreign terrorists who reportedly plot the murder of hundreds of British civilians cannot be deported back to their countries of origin, nor may they be detained here. Murderers and rapists are entitled to have any decision to keep them in prison reviewed by a judicial hearing, at which they must be represented by a lawyer – and as a result, an intimidated Probation Service frees killers who go on to murder fresh victims. The British public is increasingly worried by judgments whose effect is to rank the 'rights' of criminals higher than those of law-abiding citizens. As a result, the whole notion of human rights is becoming discredited. Rather than basic protections against arbitrary power, 'human rights' are now seen as legal fictions that prevent the police, the intelligence services and other government agencies from doing what they believe needs to be done in order to safeguard the nation.

until they start to become synonymous with the very concept of respect for human rights. This prisoner's claim concerning his human right to magazines was never accepted by decision makers and was simply rejected by the courts. Stories that present the Human Rights Act as 'a nutters' charter', 'crazy legislation', or 'barmy laws' on closer inspection turn out to be sensationalist. Attempts to paint human rights protection as madness remind us that the human rights project is often about securing rights for those who have been marginalized and made vulnerable. Those who conceived the idea of human rights centuries ago considered this was the outcome of rational thought, rather than neurosis, but they too were often seen as suffering from a delusion that such rights exist at all. We shall meet 'Mad Tom' Paine in a few pages. Let us now turn to consider the history of the concept of human rights.

We first need to understand that human rights are considered a special, narrow category of rights. William Edmundson's introductory book on rights distinguishes human rights from other rights by suggesting that: 'Human rights recognize

The Criminals' ~~Human~~ Rights Act 1998

1. Headline from *The Sunday Telegraph*, 14 May 2006: branding the Human Rights Act 'the refuge of terrorists and scoundrels'

extraordinarily special, basic interests, and this sets them apart from rights, even moral rights, generally.' Richard Falk suggests that human rights are a 'new type of rights' achieving prominence as a result of the adoption of the Universal Declaration of Human Rights by the United Nations in 1948. This point is worth remembering throughout the book: we are not talking about all the rights that human beings may have – we are considering a rather special category of rights.

Many who approach the subject of human rights turn to early religious and philosophical writings. In their vision of human rights, human beings are endowed, by reason of their humanity, with certain fundamental and inalienable rights. This conclusion has existed in various forms in various societies. The historic development of the concept of human rights is often associated with the evolution of Western philosophical and political principles, yet a different perspective could find reference to similar principles concerning mass education, self-fulfilment, respect for others, and the quest to contribute to others' well-being in Confucian, Hindu, or Buddhist traditions. Religious texts such as the Bible and the Koran can be read as creating not only duties but also rights. Recognition of the need to protect human freedom and human dignity is alluded to in some of the earliest codes, from Hammurabi's Code in ancient Babylon (around 1780 BCE), right through to the natural law traditions of the West, which built on the Greek Stoics and the Roman law notions of *jus gentium* (law for all peoples). Common to each of these codes is the recognition of certain universally valid principles and standards of behaviour. These behavioural standards arguably inspire human rights thinking, and may be seen as precursors to, or different expressions of, the idea of human rights – but the lineage is not as obvious as is sometimes suggested. Let us now look at some early historical invocations of the actual concept of *rights* (as opposed to decent behaviour) and the sceptical responses they evoked.

The Rights of Man and their Discontents

The standard Western account of the tradition of human rights is somewhat problematic. Early legal developments in the area of human rights are said to have emerged from the *Magna Carta* of 1215, a contract between the English King John and the Barons who were dissatisfied with the taxes being levied by the monarch. But, although this agreement guaranteed rights for a *freeman* not to be 'arrested, or detained in prison, or deprived of his freehold, or outlawed, or banished, or in any way molested... unless by lawful judgment of his peers and the law of the land', this guarantee was simply a right to trial by jury granted exclusively to property-owning men. The rights contained in the *Magna Carta* were not human rights, but rather political settlements. Human rights belong to all human beings and therefore cannot be restricted to a select group of privileged men. From a contemporary perspective, the *Magna Carta* turns out to be a rather unfortunate example of a human rights declaration. Suffice it to cite one sentence, clause 54 of the *Magna Carta* reads: 'No one shall be arrested or imprisoned on the appeal of a woman for the death of any person except her husband.'

The *English Bill of Rights* of 1689 is similarly sometimes considered a stepping stone to today's texts. Parliament declared that 'no excessive fine be imposed; nor cruel and unusual punishment [be] inflicted'. It also stated, however, 'That the subjects which are Protestants, may have arms for their defence suitable to their conditions, and as allowed by law.' Like the *Magna Carta*, the *Bill of Rights* was in fact a political settlement; this time between a Parliament and the King (who had abused the rights of Protestants), in order to vindicate 'ancient rights and liberties'.

At the same time, the work of a number of philosophers had a very concrete influence on the articulation of demands in the form of 'natural rights' or the 'rights of man'. John Locke's *Second Treatise of Government*, published in 1690, considered men in a 'state of nature' where they enjoyed 'a state of liberty', yet it was not 'a state of licence'. Locke reasoned that everyone 'is bound to preserve himself' so when his own preservation is not threatened everyone should 'as much as he can ... preserve the rest of mankind', and no one may 'take away or impair the life, or what tends to the preservation of the life, the liberty, health, limb, or goods of another'. In this way, 'men may be restrained from invading others' rights and from doing hurt to one another'. For Locke, 'every man has a right to punish the offender and be executioner of the law of nature'. Locke saw that this 'strange doctrine' was unworkable but argued that men remain in this state of nature until they consent to become members of 'some politic society'. Locke saw civil government as the remedy for men acting as their own judges to enforce the law of nature. He considered that this social contract, freely entered into, entitled the government to enforce laws for as long as the government respected the trust placed in it. Should the people be subject to the exercise by the government of arbitrary or absolute power over their 'lives, liberties, and estates' then, according to Locke, governmental power would be forfeited and devolve back to the people.

The Social Contract of Jean-Jacques Rousseau developed the idea that an individual may have a private will (*volonté particulière*) and that his private interest (*intérêt particulier*) 'may dictate to him very differently from the common interest'. Rousseau considered that 'whoever refuses to obey the general will shall be compelled to it by the whole body: this in fact only forces him to be free'. For Rousseau: 'Man loses by the social contract his *natural* liberty, and an unlimited right to all which tempts him, and which he can obtain; in return he acquires *civil* liberty, and proprietorship of all he possess.' Published in 1762, *The Social Contract* was a precursor to the French Revolution of 1789 and the ideas it expressed have had considerable influence around the world as people have sought to articulate the rights of the governors and the governed.

Thomas Paine was a radical English writer who participated in the revolutionary changes affecting America. He emigrated to America in 1774, and in 1776 produced a widely read pamphlet called *Common Sense* which attacked the idea of rule by monarchy and called for republican government and equal rights among citizens. He also worked on the 1776 Constitution of Pennsylvania and for the subsequent abolition of slavery in that state. Paine's publication, entitled *Rights of Man*, appeared in 1791 as a defence of the French Revolution in response to Edmund Burke's *Reflections on the Revolution in France*. Paine was popular with the people (one estimate suggests that various versions of *Rights of Man* sold 250,000 copies in two years). He was unpopular with the government and was convicted in his absence of seditious libel at the Guildhall in London. The crowds flocked to support his defence counsel, protesting the trampling of the 'liberty of the press'. Paine had by then already escaped to France and was rewarded with election to the National Convention for his defence of the Revolution. He was, however, later imprisoned, having angered the Jacobins for opposing the execution of the King. He himself escaped the death penalty (according to some accounts, the chalk mark was put on the wrong side of the door) and later left for America, where he died unfêted in 1809. His writings still resonate, and one does not have to look far to find bumper stickers and badges with Paine's aphorism from his *Rights of Man*: 'my country is the world, and my religion is to do good'.

2. **Thomas Paine, celebrated on a US postage stamp. Issued in 1968, this stamp was part of the 'Prominent Americans Series'**

Paine's writings were not clear on what are the actual *Rights of Man*. His rights theory builds on Locke and Rousseau, and concludes that a man deposits in the 'common stock of society' his natural right to act as his own judge to enforce the law of nature. Paine held that the 'power produced from the aggregate of natural rights ... cannot be applied to invade the natural rights which are retained in the individual'. Reading Paine reveals what it is that makes human rights such an enduring concept. Paine is sentimental about other people's suffering:

> When I contemplate the natural dignity of man; when I feel (for nature has not been kind enough to me to blunt my feelings) for the honour and happiness of its character, I become irritated at the attempt to govern mankind by force and fraud, as if they were all knaves and fools, and can scarcely avoid the disgust at those who are imposed upon.

Paine railed against Burke for failing to feel any compassion for those who had suffered in the Bastille prison and for being unaffected by the 'reality of distress'. We can see here, I would suggest, the real seeds of the human rights movement: a feeling of sympathy for the distress of others, coupled with a sense of injustice when governments resort to measures which invade the perceived natural rights of the individual.

Other philosophers have certainly contributed to our contemporary appreciation of the importance of respecting human dignity. Following the German philosopher Immanuel Kant, they have sought to derive the logic of human rights from absolute moral principles which can be generated from the following imperatives: first, that each of us has to act according to the principles that we wish other rational beings to act on; and second, that a person should never be treated as a means to an end, but rather as an end in themselves. In the words of the modern philosopher Alan Gerwith: 'agents and institutions are absolutely prohibited from degrading persons, treating them as if they had no rights or dignity'. This is often the starting point for rights theories that emphasize the importance of individual autonomy and agency as primordial values to be protected.

The modern concept of human rights is thus traditionally easily traced to the ideas and texts adopted at the end of the 18th century. It is well known that the 1776 American Declaration of Independence stated: 'We hold these truths to be self-evident, that all men are created equal; that they are endowed by their Creator with certain unalienable rights; that among these are life, liberty and the pursuit of happiness.' The French *Declaration of the Rights of Man and of the Citizen* followed in 1789, and its familiar first two articles recognized and proclaimed that 'Men are born and remain free and equal in rights' and that 'The aim of every political association is the preservation of the natural and inalienable rights of man; these rights are liberty, property, security, and resistance to oppression.' These revolutionary Declarations represent attempts to enshrine human rights as guiding principles in the constitutions of new states or polities. Still, the rights they referred to were mostly relevant only to those states in relation to their citizens, and only specific groups could benefit from their protection. The Declarations were inspired by a liberal conception of society and a belief in natural law, human reason, and universal order. Rights were believed (by men) to be the exclusive property of those possessing the capacity to exercise rational choice (a group that excluded women). Attempts by Olympe de Gouge to promote (by appealing to Queen Marie Antoinette) a *Declaration of the Rights of Women* and a 'Social Contract Between Man and Woman', regulating property and inheritance rights, fell on deaf ears. In England, Mary Wollstonecraft's *Vindication of the Rights of Woman* appealed for a revision of the French Constitution to respect the rights of women, arguing that men could not decide for themselves what they judged would be best for women. The denial of women's rights condemned women to the sphere of their families and left them 'groping in the dark' (see Box 2).

> **Box 2: Mary Wollstonecraft's dedication to Monsieur Talleyrand-Périgord**
>
> Consider – I address you as a legislator – whether, when men contend for their freedom, and to be allowed to judge for themselves respecting their own happiness, it be not inconsistent and unjust to subjugate women, even though you firmly believe that you are acting in the manner best calculated to promote their happiness? Who made man the exclusive judge, if women partake with him, the gift of reason? In this style argue tyrants of every denomination, from the weak king to the weak father of a family; they are all eager to crush reason, yet always assert that they usurp its throne only to be useful. Do you not act a similar part when you *force* all women, by denying them civil and political rights, to remain immured in their families groping in the dark? For surely, sir, you will not assert that a duty can be binding which is not founded on reason?

In the 19th century, natural rights, or the 'rights of man', became less relevant to political change, and thinkers such as Jeremy Bentham ridiculed the idea that 'All men are born free' as 'Absurd and miserable nonsense'. Bentham famously dismissed natural and imprescriptable rights as 'nonsense upon stilts', declaring that wanting something is not the same as having it. In Bentham's terms: 'hunger is not bread'. For Bentham, real rights were legal rights, and it was the role of law makers, and not natural rights advocates, to generate rights and determine their limits. Bentham considered that one was asking for trouble, inviting anarchy even, to suggest that government was constrained by natural rights.

The contemporary scholar Amartya Sen has recalled Bentham's influence, and highlighted a 'legitimacy critique' whereby some see human rights as 'pre-legal moral claims' that 'can hardly be seen as giving justiciable rights in courts and other institutions of enforcement'. Sen cautions against confusing human rights with 'legislated legal rights'. He also points to a further reaction to human rights discourse: it has been claimed by some that human rights are alien to some cultures which may prefer to prioritize other principles, such as respect for authority. Sen calls this the 'cultural critique'. This last criticism is a common preoccupation of commentators whenever the topic of human rights is raised. Indeed, *The Very Short Introduction to Empire* suggests that, for some observers, the International Criminal Tribunal for the former Yugoslavia (well known for the aborted trial of Slobodan Milošović) is an imperialist creation, and that for 'such critics, the whole idea of "universal" human rights is actually a gigantic fraud, where Western imperialist or ex-colonial powers try to pass off their own, very specific and localized, idea of what "rights" should be as universal, trampling roughly over everyone else's beliefs and traditions'.

Karl Marx responded to the proclamation of rights in the Constitutions of Pennsylvania and New Hampshire and in the French Declaration by deriding the idea that rights could be useful in creating a new political community. For Marx, these rights stressed the individual's egoistic preoccupations, rather than providing human emancipation from religion, property, and law. Marx had a vision of a future community in which all needs would be satisfied, and in which there would be no conflicts of interests and, therefore, no role for rights or their enforcement. Marx also highlighted the puzzle that if rights can be limited for the public good then the proclamation that the aim of political life is the protection of rights becomes convoluted (see Box 3). We return to the issue of how to balance individual interests with the public good when we consider in Chapter 5 how modern human rights law allows for some limitations that are 'necessary in a democratic society'.

Is the story of human rights then simply a dispute between those who believe and those who doubt? Do different people, depending on their situations, perceive rights as either helpful for their struggle or as bourgeois obstacles to revolutionary change? Are

> ### Box 3: Karl Marx, On the Jewish Question
>
> It is puzzling enough that a people which is just beginning
> to liberate itself, to tear down all the barriers between its
> various sections, and to establish a political community, that
> such a people solemnly proclaims (Declaration of 1791) the
> rights of egoistic man separated from his fellow men and from
> the community, and that indeed it repeats this proclamation
> at a moment when only the most heroic devotion can save
> the nation, and is therefore imperatively called for, at a
> moment when the sacrifice of all the interests of civil society
> must be the order of the day, and egoism must be punished
> as a crime. (Declaration of the Rights of Man, etc., of 1793.)
> This fact becomes still more puzzling when we see that the
> political emancipators go so far as to reduce citizenship, and
> the *political community*, to a mere *means* for maintaining
> these so-called rights of man, that therefore the *citoyen* is
> declared to be the servant of egoistic *homme*, that the sphere
> in which man acts as a communal being is degraded to a level
> below the sphere in which he acts as a partial being, and that,
> finally, it is not man as *citoyen*, but man as *bourgeois* who is
> considered to be the *essential* and *true* man.

rights enthusiasts and their critics in perpetual antagonism?
Modern rights theorists have sought to justify the existence and
importance of rights by reference to some overriding value, such
as freedom, autonomy, or equality. Such philosophical excursions
are helpful because they tell us *why* we might want to protect
human rights. We can see that rights can be instrumental to build
a society that allows people the freedom to develop as autonomous
individuals, while allowing participation based on equality in the
community's decision-making process. In other words, we can
start to admit that political arrangements are useful for protecting
human rights, not because every community must be about
protecting God-given rights, but rather because human rights

seem to prove a useful way to protect other values, such as dignity and participatory democracy.

Some philosophers have suggested that we abandon the quest for a convincing theory of why we have human rights. For Richard Rorty, it is a fact that: 'the emergence of the human rights culture seems to owe nothing to increased moral knowledge, and everything to hearing sad and sentimental stories', and that we should put foundationalist moral theories concerned with human rights behind us so that we can better 'concentrate our energies on manipulating sentiments, on sentimental education'.

Lively discussion continues about the utility of human rights for progressive change. Many question whether adopting a rights strategy might not result in entrenching existing property interests. Feminists continue to highlight the failure of human rights to address structural inequality between the sexes, issues of private violence against women, and the need for greater inclusion of women in decision making. Even reorienting human rights to address these issues could be considered simply a measure to reinforce stereotypes of women as victims of violence and in need of protection. At another level, as references to human rights feature increasingly in the discourse of Western leaders, some fear that human rights are becoming instrumentalized, deployed as excuses for intervention by powerful countries in the political, economic, and cultural life of weaker countries from the South. This level of criticism does not seek to deny that human rights exist. Indeed, human rights are under attack today, not because of doubts about their existence, but rather due to their omnipresence. Let us leave moral philosophy for now and see what insights we can glean from the way human rights have sometimes been portrayed in 20th-century literature.

Kundera on human rights

The language of international human rights has become associated with all sorts of claims and disputes. Almost everyone now emphasizes their point of view in terms of an assertion or denial of rights. Indeed, for some in the West, it seems we have already entered an era when rights talk is becoming banal. Let us illustrate this with an excerpt from Milan Kundera's story 'The gesture of protest against a violation of human rights'. The story centres on Brigitte, who, following an argument with her German teacher (over the absence of logic in German grammar), drives through Paris to buy a bottle of wine from Fauchon.

> She wanted to park but found it impossible: rows of cars parked bumper to bumper lined the pavements for a radius of half a mile; after circling round and round for fifteen minutes, she was overcome with indignant astonishment at the total lack of space; she drove the car onto the pavement, got out and set out for the store.

As she approached the store she noticed something strange. Fauchon is a very expensive store, but on this occasion it was overrun by about 100 unemployed people all 'poorly dressed'. In Kundera's words:

> It was a strange protest: the unemployed did not come to break anything or to threaten anyone or to shout slogans; they just wanted to embarrass the rich, and by their mere presence to spoil their appetite for wine and caviar.

Brigitte succeeded in getting her bottle of wine and returned to her car to find two policemen asking her to pay a parking fine. Brigitte started to abuse the policemen and when they pointed to the fact that the car was illegally parked and blocking the pavement, Brigitte pointed to all the rows of cars parked one behind the other:

> 'Can you tell me where I was supposed to park? If people are permitted to buy cars, they should also be guaranteed a place to put them, right? You must be logical!' she shouted at them.

Kundera tells the story to focus on the following detail:

> at the moment when she was shouting at the policemen, Brigitte
> recalled the unemployed demonstrators in Fauchon's and felt a
> strong sense of sympathy for them: she felt united with them in a
> common fight. That gave her courage and she raised her voice; the
> policeman (hesitant, just like the women in fur coats under the gaze
> of the unemployed) kept repeating in an unconvincing and foolish
> manner words such as forbidden, prohibited, discipline, order, and
> in the end let her off without a fine.

Kundera tells us that during the dispute Brigitte kept rapidly
shaking her head from left to right and at the same time lifting her
shoulders and eyebrows. She again shakes her head from left to
right when she tells the story to her father. Kundera writes:

> We have encountered this movement before: it expresses indignant
> astonishment at the fact that someone wants to deny us our most
> self-evident rights. Let us therefore call this *the gesture of protest
> against a violation of human rights*.

For Kundera, it is the contradiction between the French
revolutionary proclamations of rights and the existence of
concentration camps in Russia that triggered the relatively recent
Western enthusiasm for human rights:

> The concept of human rights goes back some two hundred years,
> but it reached its greatest glory in the second half of the 1970s.
> Alexander Solzhenitsyn had just been exiled from his country and
> his striking figure, adorned with beard and handcuffs, hypnotized
> Western intellectuals sick with a longing for the great destiny which
> had been denied them. It was only thanks to him that they started
> to believe, after a fifty-year delay, that in communist Russia there
> were concentration camps; even progressive people were now ready
> to admit that imprisoning someone for his opinions was not just.
> And they found an excellent justification for their new attitude:

Russian communists violated human rights, in spite of the fact that these rights had been gloriously proclaimed by the French Revolution itself!

And so, thanks to Solzhenitsyn, human rights once again found their place in the vocabulary of our times. I don't know a single politician who doesn't mention 10 times a day 'the fight for human rights' or 'violations of human rights'. But because people in the West are not threatened by concentration camps and are free to say and write what they want, the more the fight for human rights gains in popularity the more it loses any concrete content, becoming a kind of universal stance of everyone towards everything, a kind of energy that turns all human desires into rights. The world has become man's right and everything in it has become a right: the desire for love the right to love, the desire for rest the right to rest, the desire for friendship the right to friendship, the desire to exceed the speed limit to right to exceed the speed limit, the desire for happiness the right to happiness, the desire to publish a book the right to publish a book, the desire to shout in the street in the middle of the night the right to shout in the street. The unemployed have the right to occupy an expensive food store, the women in fur coats have the right to buy caviar, Brigitte has the right to park on the pavement and everybody, the unemployed, the women in fur coats as well as Brigitte, belongs to the same army of fighters for human rights.

Kundera's essay makes a few points about the changing world of human rights. First, for some people today, human rights are obvious, self-evident, and simply logical. There is often no challenge regarding the source of these rights or even the theoretical foundations of a rights claim. The foundations of the rights regime seem to us so solid that the act of invoking rights in itself seems to make you right.

Second, human rights are claims that automatically occur to one once one feels hard done by. A sense of injustice can breed a feeling that one has been denied one's rights. Appeals to rights as derived through irrefutable logic and entitlement are today somehow more immediately convincing than concepts such as 'social contract', 'the law of nature', or 'right reason'. Brigitte convinces the police through an appeal to a logical entitlement to a *right* to park on the pavement. An appeal for generosity, forgiveness, humanity, or charity would have involved a different gesture.

Third, a shared sense of grievance provides powerful succour for those claiming their 'rights'. When those of us who feel aggrieved stand together in protest we find strength through solidarity. The law itself may be the target of the protest. Outrage at law can somehow delegitimize such laws even in the eyes of law enforcers. Obedience to the law is a habit often related to the law's reasonableness. Invoking our human rights has become a way to challenge laws that we feel are unjust (even when the law has been adopted according to the correct procedures). In fact, human rights law has now developed so that, in almost all states, national law can be challenged for its lack of conformity with human rights. As laws are repealed and struck down, there is a valid perception that the legitimacy, or even legality, of all law has to be judged against human rights law. The hierarchy between human (or constitutional) rights law and normal national law is now mirrored at the international level in the hierarchy between general international law and certain 'superior' international law prohibitions (known as 'peremptory' or *'jus cogens'* norms). Human rights operate from a higher plane and are used to criticize normal laws.

Fourth, appealing to rights and ensuring respect for rights is a way of, not only achieving a fixed goal, but changing the system we live in. Human rights are important as instruments for change in the world. Human rights have moved on from the idea of citizens' individual entitlements in a national revolutionary proclamation (such as the French Declaration of 1789 or the political settlements contained in the *Magna Carta* of 1215). Today, not only are human rights claims instrumental in changing national law, but human rights principles have also become relevant to designing international development assistance projects, evaluating lending conditions and project designs of the international financial institutions, facilitating transitions from communist to market economies, rebuilding war-torn societies, and combating poverty.

Fifth, for some there is an historical association between human rights and Western preoccupations, and it has therefore been tempting to dismiss those who raise the issue of human rights as divorced from the actual deprivations they are talking about. The example of a rich girl complaining about lack of parking space is of course deliberately absurd and ironic. But Kundera's story illustrates how human rights outrage can quickly be made to seem ridiculous, even hypocritical, as certain Western governments selectively sanction and support human rights violations. It would, however, be a mistake to overemphasize the association of human rights with Western hypocrisy. In fact, the modern human rights movement and the complex normative international framework have grown out of a number of transnational and widespread movements. Human rights were invoked and claimed in the contexts of anti-colonialism, anti-imperialism, anti-slavery, anti-apartheid, anti-racism, and feminist and indigenous struggles everywhere. Western governments may recently have dominated the discourse at the highest international levels, but the chanting on the ground did not necessarily take its cue from them, nor did it sing to the West's tune.

Sixth, the sense of solidarity amongst those who believe they are the victims of a human rights violation can transcend class, gender, and other distinctions. This sense of connectedness is critical to understanding the changing world of human rights. Part of the justification for the primacy of certain human rights norms in public international law is that certain acts offend the conscience of humanity. It is the sense of common humanity and shared suffering that keeps the world of human rights moving and explains the *gesture of protest against a violation of human rights*.

Lastly, through the eyes of Kundera and Brigitte we observe several different logics of human rights depending on culture, time, place, and knowledge. This is a European story. There are African, Asian, or American stories which would be very different. But we suggest that Kundera helps us here because he identifies this special contemporary gesture as an internal human feeling which drives the discourse. The vocabulary of human rights is not a simple revelation of a deep universal structure which we all innately understand. Nor is it a language to be learned as an adult. It is the story of struggles concerning injustice, inhumanity, and better government. And at the same time, the world of human rights provides the tools for states to pursue foreign policy goals. Unless we understand some of the driving forces behind human rights we risk missing the currents which will determine its future direction. Kundera's scepticism may jar – but it also strikes a chord. The contradiction between our commitment to the 'obvious' moral logic of human rights, and our cynicism towards certain rights claims has to be addressed head-on if we want to understand the world of human rights today.

Limits to rights reasoning

Having considered what makes human rights language resonate, let us now examine further aspects of the backlash against rights. We saw earlier how the popular media in Britain were blaming human rights for prioritizing criminals' rights over the rights of the law-abiding citizen to be safe and free from crime. In the United States, emphasis on rights is sometimes seen as undermining participatory politics. Mary Anne Glendon's book *Rights Talk: The Impoverishment of Political Discourse* asks a series of questions about whether the elevation of rights has been at the expense of citizens taking responsibility for a vital political life.

> The prevailing consensus about the goodness of rights widespread, though it may be, is thin and brittle. In truth, there is very little argument regarding *which* needs, goods, interests, or values should be characterized as 'rights,' or concerning what should be done when, as is usually the case, various rights are in tension or collision with one another. Occasions for conflict among rights multiply as catalogs of rights grow longer. If some rights are more important than others, and if a rather small group of rights is of especially high importance, then an ever expanding list of rights may well trivialize this essential core without materially advancing the proliferating causes that have been reconceptualized as involving rights.

But perhaps the problem Glendon wants to address is more closely connected, not so much to the need to protect the value of core rights against devaluation, but to the way that rights are perceived by some as absolutes. The penchant for seeing rights as winning ploys for arguments about freedom is nicely illustrated by Glendon:

> The exaggerated absoluteness of our American rights rhetoric is closely bound up with its other distinctive traits – a near silence concerning responsibility, and a tendency to envision the rights-bearer as a lone autonomous individual. Thus, for example, those who contest the legitimacy of mandatory automobile seat-belt or motor-cycle helmet laws frequently say: 'It's my body and I have the right to do as I please with it.' In this shibboleth, the old horse of property is harnessed to the service of unlimited liberty. The implication is that no one else is affected by my exercise of the individual rights in question. This way of thinking and speaking ignores the fact that it is a rare driver, passenger, or biker who does not have a child, or a spouse, or a parent. It glosses over the likelihood that if the rights-bearer comes to grief, the cost of

his medical treatment, or rehabilitation, or long-term care will be spread among many others. The independent individualist, helmetless and free on the open road, becomes the most dependent of individuals in the spinal injury ward. In the face of such facts, why does our rhetoric of rights so often shut out relationship and responsibility, along with reality?

This is a reminder of the fact that not everyone agrees that emphasizing individual rights as a way to organize society is the best way to ensure a fair distribution of opportunities, wealth, and development. Some would prefer to emphasize the need to create a sense of responsibility and community among individuals. Others, as we started to see with Marx, believe that focusing on rights dissuades us from radical changes to the *status quo*, redistributive policies, and collective arrangements for the general good (and especially for the least well off) (see Box 4).

But we have slipped back into talking about 'rights' rather than the specific category 'human rights'. This is a recurring challenge in an introduction to human rights: the origins of contemporary human rights lie in the natural, constitutional, and political rights discourses that emerged in the Enlightenment and found their way into the constitutions of the 18th and 19th centuries. Let us therefore try to disentangle modern human rights from all this 'rights talk'.

Box 4: 'An Essay on Rights' by Mark Tushnet

People need food and shelter right now, and demanding that those needs be satisfied – whether or not satisfying them can today persuasively be characterized as enforcing a right – strikes me as more likely to succeed than claiming that existing rights to food and shelter must be enforced.

Chapter 2
The historical development of international human rights

When governments, activists, or United Nations documents refer to 'human rights' today they are almost certainly referring to the human rights recognized in international and national law rather than rights in a moral or philosophical sense. Of course, philosophical debate will continue to illuminate (or sometimes obscure) the reasons *why* we think human rights are important and *how* to best develop them. But for the moment, the *content* of human rights is usually understood by reference to the legal catalogue of human rights we find developed through international texts. This legal approach responds to demands for the concrete protection of inherent natural rights, and goes some way to meeting the criticism that we are simply talking about desires and selfishness. The shift to positive law also fixes these rights in an agreed written form. Hersch Lauterpacht's influential book *An International Bill of the Rights of Man*, published in 1945, drew on a range of natural rights thinking and constitutionally protected rights to argue for a written Bill of Rights to be protected through the UN.

The key text for us today is the Universal Declaration of Human Rights, adopted by the UN General Assembly in 1948 (see Annex). But the enumeration of human rights was not simply frozen by proclamation in 1948. Since that time dozens of treaties (agreements that create binding legal obligations for states) and intergovernmental Declarations have supplemented this proclamation of rights. In 1984, at the height of this flurry of writing up rights, Philip Alston suggested that new international human rights be subjected, like wine, to a 'quality control' by the UN General Assembly. The relevant UN resolution, adopted in 1986, suggested that international human rights instruments should:

(a) Be consistent with the existing body of international human rights law;
(b) Be of fundamental character and derive from the inherent dignity and worth of the human person;
(c) Be sufficiently precise to give rise to identifiable and practicable rights and obligations;
(d) Provide where appropriate, realistic and effective implementation machinery, including reporting systems;
(e) Attract broad international support.

Some may feel that some texts have failed this test, but, overall, the UN's core human rights instruments satisfy these criteria. Let us look in more detail at the development of this human rights catalogue.

The historical development of the international protection of human rights deserves our attention as it tells us much about how and why states use human rights in international relations. The human rights story in the 20th century has multiple layers. At one level, human rights were invoked as a rationale for fighting the world wars. In 1915, in the context of World War I, Sir Francis Younghusband set up an organization called the Fight for Right movement; one of its declared aims was 'To impress upon the country that we are fighting for something more than our own defence, that we are fighting the battle of all Humanity and to preserve Human Rights for generations to come.' At another, rather more academic level, the Chilean legal scholar Alejandro Alvarez, the Secretary General of the American Institute of

International Law, was promoting in 1917 consideration of international recognition of rights for individual persons and associations.

In his 1918 address to Congress, President Wilson spoke of his desire 'to create a world dedicated to justice and fair dealing'. His ideas were expanded in a proposed 'Fourteen Points' programme, which included explicit reference to rights to self-determination and statehood for nationalities seeking autonomy. Wilson's Fourteen Points formed the basis of the Versailles Peace Treaty in 1919, which established the League of Nations and the International Labour Organization. The League was supposed to preserve international peace and security through the collective action of its member states against any state that resorted to war or the threat of war. Three developments are relevant: the minorities treaties, the development of international workers' rights, and the work on the abolition of slavery.

The Allied Powers and various Eastern European countries entered into a series of minority treaties and declarations for the protection of certain minority rights in Albania, Austria, Bulgaria, Czechoslovakia, Estonia, Finland, Greece, Hungary, Latvia, Lithuania, Poland, Romania, Turkey, and Yugoslavia. It was felt that with the redrawing of borders and the creation of new states, one should guard against the mistreatment of minorities in order to avoid disturbing the new 'peace of the world'. These treaties signalled the first multilateral efforts to protect the rights of specific groups of people at the international level. The treaties all contained similar provisions guaranteeing the protection of minority rights in the states party to the treaty, including the right to life and liberty for all inhabitants and civil and political rights for nationals.

These League of Nations efforts to legally recognize and protect minority rights were an important development, as on the one hand, they signalled attempts to protect individual rights through international law, and, on the other hand, they rebutted the argument that the way a state treats its inhabitants is not a subject of legitimate international concern. Yet, despite its important contribution to the protection of minority rights, the human rights protection offered under the League system was obviously limited to certain groups and certain countries.

The League of Nations was also active in the protection of workers' rights. The goal of 'fair and humane conditions of labour for men, women and children' was stated explicitly in the League Covenant. This goal became central to the work of the International Labour Organization (ILO), which continues today as one of the UN's specialized agencies. While the minorities treaties and the development of workers' rights can be seen as embryonic stages of the development of international human rights, we should be aware that these arrangements were put in place by governments *in their states' interests*. The human rights of individuals were granted legal protection on the basis of the individuals' ties to a state, and in order to reduce political tensions among states that might lead to war. Workers' rights were to be recognized and protected, as this was seen by some states as the best way to prevent their populations from turning to communism and to reduce the risk of revolution.

At the Paris Peace Conference in 1919 various delegates made proposals for the inclusion of respect for equality rights in the Covenant of the League of Nations. There was concern both for religious freedom and to ensure non-discrimination on the basis of race or nationality. The British delegate, Lord Cecil, even proposed that states have a right of 'intervention' against other states if these states engaged in forms of religious intolerance that would jeopardize global peace. The delegate of Japan, Baron Makino, the Foreign Minister, specifically proposed the inclusion of a sentence that would have bound the member states to agree as soon as possible to accord equal and just treatment to alien nationals of League member states without distinction based on nationality or race.

Neither of these last two proposals was adopted. With regard to the failure to include a non-discrimination provision in the League Covenant, Antonio Cassese has concluded:

> the Western great powers neither would nor could accept
> a principle that would have encroached heavily on their
> discriminatory practices against citizens of other areas of the world,
> and would have ended up threatening even the similar practices
> they still tolerated within their own systems (I have in mind above
> all, of course, racial discrimination in the United States).

We should briefly mention here the fight to outlaw the slave trade and to abolish slavery. Efforts to combat slavery had been ongoing in the 19th century. Although strategic and economic forces played a role in the abolition of slavery, there was also a genuine sentiment that slavery was inhuman; non-governmental organizations such as the Anti-Slavery Society (now Anti-Slavery International) lobbied for international action, and the fight against slavery is sometimes seen as the beginning of the human rights movement. The League set up Commissions on slavery, adopted the 1926 Slavery Convention, and developed conventions on the traffic in women and children to suppress what had been called in a 1910 Convention the 'White Slave Traffic'.

Sadly, nearly 100 years later the international human rights community is still addressing what are now called 'contemporary forms of slavery' (such as trafficking in persons and forced labour). The older international norms against slavery have been at the core of the international criminalization of trafficking, as well as central to the settlements in the 1990s regarding forced labour during the Second World War. More recently, these rights have been at the crux of the litigation brought in the US Federal Courts by villagers from Myanmar (Burma) against oil companies accused of complicity with the military authorities' forcing of the villagers to build pipelines. In 2005, the Unocal company came to an out-of-court settlement with the villagers, and provided an undisclosed sum that is to be used to compensate the villagers and to develop programmes 'to improve living conditions, health care and education and protect the rights of people from the pipeline region'.

With the League of Nations we have strategic concern for certain national minorities, attention to the plight of workers, and paternalistic worries about women engaged in prostitution. We do not yet have meaningful international rights or obligations which protect human beings as human beings.

In the inter-war period there was some interest in developing the scope of international law to cover concern for individual rights. Albert de Lapradelle, a professor of international law at the University of Paris, presented the *Institut de droit international* (the Institute of International Law) with a draft 'Declaration of the International Rights of Man'. Influenced by the League of Nations minorities treaties, de Lapradelle sought to create a text that would be universal in nature whilst appealing to all states in the international community. André Mandelstam, a professor from Russia, developed a text that formed the basis of the eventual Declaration. Importantly, the final Declaration, approved in 1929 at a meeting of the distinguished members of the Institute in New York, did not refer to the rights of *citizens* (which were a matter of domestic law and policy) but rather proclaimed rights to life, liberty, and property belonging to individual human beings. These rights are to be respected without any discrimination on grounds of nationality, sex, race, language, or religion. This text, however, remained the work of distinguished lawyers – key governments remained unenthusiastic about the international protection of human rights. In 1933, the delegate of Haiti, Antoine Frangulis, argued that states' obligations should go beyond the category of minorities and be extended through a general convention, to offer the same protection and freedoms to everyone. Such a proposal did not suit powerful states. The historian Paul Lauren quotes a British official, who said 'he did not wish to be quoted', as having said 'the acceptance of such a proposal by His Majesty's Government would be entirely impossible in view of our colonial experience'.

Almost from the beginning of the Second World War we find human rights being invoked. In 1939, the British author H. G. Wells wrote to *The Times* of London arguing for a discussion of the War Aims. He suggested the League of Nations was 'a poor and ineffective outcome of that revolutionary proposal to banish armed conflict from the world and inaugurate a new life for mankind'. Wells was 'terrified' of a repetition of the 'Geneva simulacrum'. In a follow-up letter, he appended a Declaration of Rights to define the spirit in which 'our people are more or less consciously fighting', as well as 'to appeal very forcibly to every responsive spirit under the yoke of the obscurantist and totalitarian tyrannies with which we are in conflict'. In other words, Wells considered these rights had universal appeal and gave sense to the fighting. This Declaration was developed into the *World Declaration of the Rights of Man*, and distributed to over 300 editors in 48 countries, generating worldwide interest. The ten paragraphs covered: discrimination; natural resources; health; education; paid employment; the right to buy and sell personal property; the right to move around the world freely; no imprisonment longer than six days without charge, and then no more than three months before a public trial; access to public records concerning individuals; and a prohibition on mutilation, sterilization, torture, and any bodily punishment.

The Declaration was included in Wells's widely distributed 1940 Penguin Special entitled *The Rights of Man: or what are we fighting for?* The book contained other declarations of rights, including a 1936 '*Complément à la Déclaration des Droits de l'homme*' prepared by the *Ligue des Droits de l'homme*.

A PENGUIN SPECIAL

What are we fighting for?

H. G. WELLS

ON

THE RIGHTS OF MAN

3. The H. G. Wells paperback; the Allies are said to have dropped the Declaration behind enemy lines. Wells's *Declaration of Rights* was widely distributed and translated into not only European languages but also into Chinese, Japanese, Arabic, Urdu, Hindi, Bengali, Gujerati, Hausa, Swahili, Yoruba, Zulu, and Esperanto

Wells expressed the concern that laws were being passed that were disproportionate to the threats posed by traitors and foreigners (see Box 5). Interestingly, these concerns are remarkably relevant to present-day debates about terrorists, refugees, and others. The revised version of Wells's publication, the 1942 *Rights of the World Citizen*, ended with the following appeal:

> These are the rights of all human beings. They are yours whoever you are. Demand that your rulers and politicians sign and observe this declaration. If they refuse, if they quibble, they can have no place in the new free world that dawns upon mankind.

So the horrors of the Second World War provided this impetus for the modern human rights movement. Wells discussed his Declaration with a variety of people, and most importantly with those who were being asked to fight. Their concern was not only to 'put down violence' but more significantly 'they had been stirred profoundly by those outrages upon human dignity perpetrated by the Nazis'.

In 1941, in a related (but not necessarily connected) move, US President Franklin Roosevelt famously proclaimed, in his annual State of the Union address to Congress, four essential human

Box 5: H. G. Wells, *The Rights of Man: or what are we fighting for?*

... there has accumulated a vast tangle of emergency legislation, regulations, barriers and restraints, out of all proportion to and often missing and distorting the needs of the situation. For the restoration and modernisation of human civilisation, this exaggerated outlawing of the fellow citizen whom we see fit to suspect as a traitor or revolutionary and also of the stranger within our gates, has to be restrained and brought back within the scheme of human rights.

freedoms: freedom of speech, freedom of worship, freedom from want, and freedom from fear. The speech also explained that: 'Freedom means the supremacy of human rights everywhere.' During the same year, President Roosevelt and Prime Minister Churchill issued a joint declaration known now as the 'Atlantic Charter', which set out their vision for the post-war world. The joint declaration stated that:

> after the final destruction of the Nazi tyranny, they hope to see established a peace which will afford to all nations the means of dwelling in safety within their own boundaries, and which will afford assurance that all the men in all the lands may live out their lives in freedom from fear and want.

In turn, representatives of 26 Allied nations later signed a Declaration by United Nations on 1 January 1942, subscribing to the purposes and principles in the Atlantic Charter and stating that they were:

> convinced that complete victory over their enemies is essential to defend life, liberty, independence and religious freedom, and to preserve human rights and justice in their own lands as well as in other lands, and that they are now engaged in a common struggle against savage and brutal forces seeking to subjugate the world.

In addition to the Allied nations at war with the Axis powers, a further 21 states had also signed the Declaration by August 1945. This combined group would become the core of the 51 original member states of the United Nations Organization. The UN Charter adopted in 1945 commits the Organization to encouraging respect for human rights and obligates the member states to cooperate with the UN for the promotion of universal respect for, and observance of, human rights. However, efforts to include a legally binding bill of rights at that time came to nothing. Instead, the immediate focus was on the prosecution of international crimes.

Prosecution of international crimes

At the end of the Second World War, the victorious powers established the Nuremberg International Military Tribunal to try the 'major war criminals of the European Axis' and the Tokyo Tribunal to try the 'major war criminals in the Far East'. These two Tribunals tried individuals for crimes against peace (aggression), war crimes, and crimes against humanity (in connection with aggression or war crimes). The Nuremberg Tribunal sentenced 12 defendants to death, and five defendants to long sentences of imprisonment. The Tokyo Tribunal sentenced seven defendants to death and 16 received life sentences. For some, the purpose of these trials was to demonstrate that the Allies were better than the Fascists, and to serve an educational purpose. However, the trials can also be seen in other ways. From one perspective, they represented victor's justice: war crimes which may have been committed by the Allies were beyond the jurisdiction of the Tribunals, and the charges of crimes against peace and crimes against humanity seemed to rest on rather uncertain legal ground.

From another perspective, the Nuremberg judgment initiated a new way of thinking about international law and its impact on the individual. The defendants were seen as having violated the international law of war, a law that could be gleaned from general principles of justice applied by military courts. The Tribunal declared: 'This law is not static, but by continual adaptation follows the needs of a changing world.' The Tribunal went on to dismiss any notion that this law was confined to duties for states or that individuals could hide behind traditional notions of state immunity: 'Crimes against international law are committed by men, not by abstract entities, and only by punishing individuals who commit such crimes can the provisions of international law be enforced.' Furthermore, the development of the category of crimes referred to as 'crimes against humanity' finally cemented the idea that international obligations are owed to individuals because of their human worth, rather than because they are protected abroad by their state of nationality, or are protected through an *ad hoc* treaty protecting national minorities.

This concept of crimes against humanity in international law can be traced back to a 1915 Joint Declaration by France, Great Britain, and Russia concerning the Armenians. The diplomatic exchanges show that the original Russian draft declaration referred to crimes 'against Christianity and civilization'. The French were, however, worried that care should be taken that the Muslim population living under French and British rule would not conclude that the interests of these two powers led to action only when Christians were threatened. The British concurred that the phrase could be omitted. The Imperial Russian Foreign Ministry had been appealed to by the Armenian *Dachnaksoutiun* 'for the love of humanity' to hold the members of the government individually responsible. Rather than omitting the phrase, the Russians successfully proposed to replace 'Christianity' with 'humanity'. The final Declaration referred to specific sites and stated that in view 'of those new crimes of Turkey against humanity and civilization', the Allied governments would 'hold personally responsible' all those 'implicated in such massacres'. In fact, the promise by Turkey in 1920 to hand over those persons whom the Allies considered responsible for the massacres was contained in a treaty that never entered into force, and the later 1923 peace treaty included a declaration of amnesty.

The category of crimes against humanity was used in the 1945 Nuremberg Charter to ensure that the deportation *of Germans* by Germans to the concentration camps, and their subsequent mistreatment and extermination, could be prosecuted. Under the international laws of war at that time, the way in which a government treated its own nationals (no matter how heinous) was considered by international law as exclusively a matter of *domestic* jurisdiction, rather than an issue of international concern. The concept of crimes against humanity was therefore used to include these atrocities as part of the international prosecution. The Allies were, however, careful to ensure that crimes against humanity were included only to the extent they were connected to the war. At the time, this was to ensure the concept could not be easily extended to prosecute those who might be accused of mistreating the inhabitants of the colonies or the United States.

The General Assembly adopted the *Convention on the Prevention and Punishment of the Crime of Genocide* on 9 December 1948 to remedy the limitations of the concept of crimes against humanity used in the Nuremberg Tribunal (see Box 6). The Convention declares that genocide is a crime under international law whether committed in time of peace or of war. It defines genocide as any of

---

Box 6: W. A. Schabas, *Preventing Genocide and Mass Killing: The Challenge for the United Nations**

In October 1946, only days after the judgment of the Nuremberg Tribunal, Cuba, India, Panama and Saudi Arabia demanded that the first session of the General Assembly correct the limitation on the concept of crimes against humanity that the four great powers had imposed. They proposed this be done not by redefining crimes against humanity in order to eliminate the nexus with armed conflict but by acknowledging the existence of a cognate concept, the international crime of genocide. There was a price to pay, however, to get the great powers to agree with liability for atrocities committed against their own populations in time of peace, something they had refused for crimes against humanity. The first was the narrowness of the definition of the crime of genocide. The categories contemplated for the crime of genocide were limited to 'national, ethnical, racial or religious' groups, whereas crimes against humanity covered other forms of discriminatory criteria, such as political groups.

---

the following acts committed with intent to destroy, in whole or in part, a national, ethnical, racial or religious group, as such:

(a) Killing members of the group;

(b) Causing serious bodily or mental harm to members of the group;

(c) Deliberately inflicting on the group conditions of life calculated to bring about its physical destruction in whole or in part;

(d) Imposing measures intended to prevent births within the group;

(e) Forcibly transferring children of the group to another group.

Conceived in the context of the Holocaust by Raphael Lemkin, a determined Jewish lawyer from Poland, the concept of genocide was enshrined in the new Convention to create obligations on states to prevent and punish genocide. Importantly, the Convention makes the individual perpetrator punishable 'whether they are constitutionally responsible rulers, public officials, or private individuals'. The Convention has been central to the work of the *ad hoc* international criminal tribunals established by the Security Council to deal with crimes committed in the former Yugoslavia and in Rwanda.

The former Prime Minister of Rwanda, Jean Kambanda, was sentenced to life imprisonment for genocide and crimes against humanity. Radislav Krstic, Chief of Staff of the Bosnian Serb Army (Drina Corps), was sentenced to 35 years' imprisonment for aiding and abetting genocide in Srebrenica by allowing military personnel under his command to be used for the murder of about 8,000 men (see Box 7).

Even if crimes against humanity were generally seen as something different from human rights, today genocide and other crimes against humanity are increasingly seen as part of the human rights story. By 1991, the terms were intermingled by the

> **Box 7: International Criminal Tribunal for the former Yugoslavia *Krstic* case**
>
> By seeking to eliminate a part of the Bosnian Muslims, the Bosnian Serb forces committed genocide. They targeted for extinction the forty thousand Bosnian Muslims living in Srebrenica, a group which was emblematic of the Bosnian Muslims in general. They stripped all the male Muslim prisoners, military and civilian, elderly and young, of their personal belongings and identification, and deliberately and methodically killed them solely on the basis of their identity. The Bosnian Serb forces were aware, when they embarked on this genocidal venture, that the harm they caused would continue to plague the Bosnian Muslims. The Appeals Chamber states unequivocally that the law condemns, in appropriate terms, the deep and lasting injury inflicted, and calls the massacre at Srebrenica by its proper name: genocide. Those responsible will bear this stigma, and it will serve as a warning to those who may in future contemplate the commission of such a heinous act.

International Law Commission in its draft *Code of Crimes against the Peace and Security of Mankind* when it used the expression 'systematic or mass violations of human rights' as the title of the article that was to become 'crimes against humanity' in 1996.

This developing recognition that certain violations of human rights could be prosecuted under international law was reflected in the lists of crimes triable before the International Criminal Tribunals for the former Yugoslavia and Rwanda. The UN Security Council established these Tribunals in the 1990s as a rather belated response to the atrocities committed in the former Yugoslavia and Rwanda, respectively. This time the Tribunals were given no jurisdiction over crimes against peace but could

4. Radislav Krstic: Commander of the Drina Corps, a formation of the Bosnian Serb Army, and, later, facing charges of genocide

try individuals for three types of international crimes: genocide, crimes against humanity, and war crimes.

The International Criminal Court, which came into existence in 2002, now has jurisdiction over certain individuals for a similar set of crimes (including a long list of crimes against humanity, see Box 8). In contrast to the Tribunals mentioned above, where jurisdiction was established due to victorious occupation or a binding decision of the UN Security Council, the International Criminal Court may usually only try individuals who either have the nationality of a state that has accepted to be bound by the Court's Statute, or who have committed their crimes in such a state. There now over 100 such states, including Afghanistan, Australia, Burundi, Canada, Colombia, Democratic Republic of Congo, Germany, Italy, Jordan, Liberia, Nigeria, Peru, Senegal, Sierra Leone, Uganda, and the United Kingdom. Additionally, if the Security Council considers that a situation threatens international peace and security, it can refer that situation to the Court's Prosecutor for investigation and an eventual prosecution

5. Child soldiers in the Democratic Republic of Congo

of individuals accused of genocide, crimes against humanity, or war crimes. This happened in 2005 with regard to the situation in Dafur (Sudan). At the time of writing, the Prosecutor was also investigating crimes committed in Uganda and in the Democratic Republic of Congo. The first arrest concerned

Box 8: Statute of the International Criminal Court*

Article 7 Crimes against humanity

1. For the purpose of this Statute, 'crime against humanity' means any of the following acts when committed as part of a widespread or systematic attack directed against any civilian population, with knowledge of the attack:

(a) Murder;

(b) Extermination;

(c) Enslavement;

(d) Deportation or forcible transfer of population;

(e) Imprisonment or other severe deprivation of physical liberty in violation of fundamental rules of international law;

(f) Torture;

(g) Rape, sexual slavery, enforced prostitution, forced pregnancy, enforced sterilization, or any other form of sexual violence of comparable gravity;

(h) Persecution against any identifiable group or collectivity on political, racial, national, ethnic, cultural, religious, gender ... or other grounds that are universally recognized as impermissible under international law, in connection with any act referred to in this paragraph or any crime within the jurisdiction of the Court;

(i) Enforced disappearance of persons;

(j) The crime of apartheid;

(k) Other inhumane acts of a similar character intentionally causing great suffering, or serious injury to body or to mental or physical health.

Thomas Lubango Dyilo (allegedly from the rebel group *Union des Patriotes Congolois*) accused of war crimes including 'enlisting and coscripting children under the age of 15 and using them to particiate actively in hostilities'.

It is perhaps too early to see how the International Criminal Court will develop to protect human rights. The important point is that everyone has been put on notice that they could end up as a defendant before this court should they commit, or assist others to commit, certain international crimes that violate human rights. This has raised awareness in all quarters about what behaviour is acceptable, even in times of war. The existence of the Court is clearly not enough to stem the tide of vicious human rights violations – only a handful of people will be tried in the coming years – nevertheless, we must hope that some people in some places are dissuaded from committing human rights violations some of the time.

These international judicial arrangements are not without their critics. On the one hand, the US Government has opposed the International Criminal Court until it can be sure that it will be impossible for the Court to sit in judgment on US citizens. On the other hand, following the publicity given to the International Court's arrest warrants for the leaders of the rebel Lord's Resistance Army in Uganda, some argued that this disrupted the peace negotiations, generated a further round of violence, and exposed potential witnesses to unacceptable risks. A further line of criticism argues that the international tribunals shift the focus away from the communities that need to come to terms with their own history and delay the development of national legal systems that can enjoy the confidence of the people. The decision to try Saddam Hussein in a Baghdad court, however, illustrates how problematic it can be to mount local prosecutions for human rights crimes. Witnesses and lawyers were intimidated and killed, the judges were subjected to political pressure, and Saddam Hussein was sentenced to be hanged by the neck until dead.

The manner of the execution itself attracted the most vehement criticism as the taunting was caught on a mobile phone camera and seen via the internet around the world.

The Universal Declaration of Human Rights

Let us leave the contemporary use of the concept of crimes against humanity and return to the end of the Second World War. The establishment of the United Nations signalled the beginning of a period of unprecedented international concern for the protection of human rights. Under the auspices of the UN, several key instruments were established for the promotion and protection of human rights. The day after the adoption of the Genocide Convention, the General Assembly proclaimed the Universal Declaration of Human Rights 'as a common standard of achievement for all peoples and all nations' (see the Annex to this book).

An evaluation of the relevance of the Universal Declaration, as it turns 60, would have to conclude that the Declaration has had a huge influence, both in terms of spreading the philosophy of human rights, and in terms of inspiring legal texts and decisions. Translated into over 300 languages, it has often been at the heart of demands made by peoples and individuals around the world that their rights be respected and protected. Several constitutions have taken its provisions as the basis for a bill of rights, and national and international courts have invoked the Declaration in their judgments. The member states of the UN have come to acknowledge that the Declaration, although not in the form of a binding legal instrument, does contain actual human rights obligations. In 1968, the Teheran International Conference (the first World Conference on Human Rights) 'solemnly' proclaimed that 'The Universal Declaration of Human Rights states a common understanding of the peoples of the world concerning the inalienable and inviolable rights of all members of the human family and constitutes an obligation for the members of the international community.' By proclaiming the Universal Declaration in 1948, and continually reaffirming the obligations that stem from it, the UN General Assembly has given an international meaning to the expression 'human rights'.

Article 1 sets out the philosophical foundations upon which the Declaration is based, using language similar to that of the French Declaration of 1789: 'All human beings are born free and equal in dignity and rights. They are endowed with reason and conscience and should act towards one another in a spirit of brotherhood.' The Declaration therefore stresses the inherent value of human dignity, which should be recognized 'without distinction of any kind'. The Declaration sets certain limitations on the exercise of human rights, recognizing the need for a social order for the full realization of the rights. Article 29 acknowledges that the individual owes certain duties to the community 'in which alone the free and full development of his personality are possible'. The limits imposed by these duties must be determined by law, and can only be for the purposes of securing due recognition and respect for the rights of others and to meet 'the just requirements of morality, public order and the general welfare in a democratic society'.

Commentators have sometimes described the vision expressed in the Declaration as 'Western', and the committee that drafted the Declaration was indeed skewed westward. Abdullahi An-Na'im has pointed out that 'the only representatives of non-Western countries in that committee were Chang Peng-Chung of China and Charles Habib Malik of Lebanon. Both had been educated in American universities, and both reflected their "westernization" in the positions they took during the debates.' But An-Na'im's point is not that greater participation by non-Western diplomats would have produced a radically different document. An-Na'im wants to stress that it was unlikely that 'those representatives could reasonably have identified with, and genuinely represented their indigenous cultural traditions at the time of the drafting and adoption of the Universal Declaration and the Covenants'. For him, the lack of concern for cultural legitimacy 'may have diminished the validity of international human rights standards as seen from non-Western cultural perspectives', while the main influences were limited to official representatives from Latin America, the Soviet Union, the United States, and Europe, and not drawn from a wider variety of cultures. Since that time the governments of new UN member states have endorsed not only the idea of human rights, but also consider the Universal Declaration as a starting point for all human rights discussion. No government currently questions the commitments contained in the Universal Declaration.

The major controversy for diplomats at the time of the Declaration's adoption was not the validity of the values contained in the Declaration, but rather the antagonism between the Socialist bloc and the West (see Boxes 9 and 10 for excerpts from speeches from delegates from the USSR and the United Kingdom). In the end, the Socialist states were unable to achieve their vision of an effective implementation of economic and social rights and abstained from the vote on the Declaration. The Western powers, while keen to trumpet their own political model as superior, were at the same time careful to ensure the Declaration had no immediate legal effect.

Are human rights now really universal? While it is true that African and Asian governments currently accept the Universal Declaration and have signed various human rights treaties, such a formalistic response fails to capture the cultural differences in the appreciation of what human rights are about, and what new obligations ought to be included in the catalogue. An-Na'im suggests that the feeling of a lack of cultural legitimacy can be addressed through a cross-cultural critique of behaviour which builds on locally accepted norms. The pressing issue is not so much whether the representatives in 1948 legitimize the claims of

> **Box 9: Mr Vyshinsky (USSR), 9 December 1948, UN General Assembly, summary records**
>
> The delegation of the USSR could not accept article 20, which did nothing to solve the question. Complete freedom to disseminate ideas did not solve the problem of freedom of expression. There were dangerous ideas the diffusion of which should be prevented, war-mongering and fascist ideas for instance ... It was no use to argue that ideas should only be opposed by other ideas; ideas had not stopped Hitler making war ... That article also made no provision for the free dissemination of just and lofty ideas. If freedom of expression was to be effective, the workers must have the means of voicing their opinions, and for that they must have at their disposal printing presses and newspapers. The USSR delegation had proposed that the article should be amended so as to give the workers the material means by which they could express themselves, but the USSR amendment had been rejected on the pleas that it might permit the State to restrict freedom of expression. For its part, the delegation of the USSR considered that the rejection of that amendment constituted an attempt to prevent the masses of the people from obtaining the means of expression which would make them independent of the capitalist or official Press.

universality, but rather how we now build a universal appreciation for these ideas.

Some governments object to the demand that human rights include the concept of 'collective rights' for indigenous peoples or minorities. This objection is based on a particular appreciation of what human rights should be about (for example, some derive human rights from the starting point that there is an imagined social contract between the *individual* and the state); it is, however, hard to square this conceptual objection with

> **Box 10: Mr Davies (UK), 10 December 1948, UN General Assembly, summary records**
>
> Mention had been made of territories in which all rights were disregarded. Such territories should not be sought among British territories, which were largely self-governing, but rather among the totalitarian States of Eastern Europe, where there was no freedom of the Press except for supporters of the Government, where justice was subordinated to political requirements, where millions of human beings were held in concentration camps and where the role of parliaments was more and more limited to ratifying the decisions of the party in power ... The development of fascism had been due more to the suppression of the freedom of expression than to the dissemination of lies. The fact that political refugees came from the East to the West of Europe proved that the same danger still existed in some countries.

the explicit recognition in Western countries of certain 'human' rights guarantees for entities such as newspapers (for freedom of expression), trade unions (for freedom of association), and companies (for respect for their property and premises). Similarly, contemporary debate about economic, social, and cultural rights is held hostage by those who consider that one cannot conceive of rights to housing, health, and education as judicially enforceable entitlements – better to see them as aspirations, public policy goals, or simply socialist rhetoric. We shall see later the extent to which human rights expert bodies have given meaning to such economic, social, and cultural rights.

So, even if there is apparent universal acceptance of the human rights message, there is still discord over what constitutes a human right and how rights should be implemented. Clearly a starting point should be enforcement at the national level. Today, in many states national laws reproduce, or give effect to, international human rights (i.e. international human rights are 'translated' into the national legal order). Needless to say, this is by no means a perfect process and many rights get 'lost in translation'.

Furthermore, as we move from lofty proclamations to detailed implementation and accountability, we encounter the reaction that rights have to be implemented according to the cultural and economic context of the country concerned. This is sometimes seen as the death knell for the credibility of the so-called 'universality' of human rights. It is, however, a mistake to imagine that human rights can, or should, operate divorced from any local context. Even the application of an accepted right, such as the right to life, can beg different interpretations depending on the context. In a recent case concerning a dispute between two estranged parents of frozen embryos, the European Court of Human Rights held that:

> in the absence of any European consensus on the scientific and legal definition of the beginning of life, the issue of when the right to life begins comes within the margin of appreciation which the Court generally considers that States should enjoy in this sphere.

The international judges were divided over the separate question of whether the destruction of the embryos constituted a violation of the mother's right to respect for her private life. Again, they considered the matter was better left to national legislators than to a judicial divination of overriding human rights principles. In different countries, the father's withdrawal of consent to implantation of an embryo has been given different weight. In the absence of 'international consensus' or 'common ground' among European states, the human rights Court found that the legislation before the Court (which required the father's consent before implantation of the embryo) was within the margin allowed by the European Convention on Human Rights. In short, human rights law does allow for different approaches to implementation across cultures and nations. At the same time, there is, of course, a sense that there is some core content to each right, and that failure to respect that content can be universally condemned.

The International Covenants

Following the adoption of the Universal Declaration, the UN's Human Rights Commission began work on a legally binding text in the form of a treaty together with measures for implementation. Governments had decided that there should be a binding multilateral treaty on human rights to complement the existing Declaration. Due to political disagreements about including all types of rights within one treaty, the General Assembly requested the Commission to draft two separate covenants – one on 'civil and political' rights, and another on 'economic, social and cultural' rights. On 16 December 1966, the General Assembly adopted the *International Covenant on Economic, Social and Cultural Rights* and the *International Covenant on Civil and Political Rights*. Both came into force in 1976.

The International Covenant on Economic, Social and Cultural Rights covers human rights in areas including education, food, housing, and health care, as well as the right to work and to just and favourable conditions of work. A state that becomes a party to the Covenant agrees to take steps for the progressive realization of Covenant rights to the full extent of that state's available resources. The International Covenant on Civil and Political Rights safeguards rights such as rights to life, liberty, fair trial, freedom of movement, thought, conscience, peaceful assembly, family, and privacy. It also prohibits slavery; torture; cruel, inhuman, or degrading treatment; and punishment, discrimination, arbitrary arrest, and imprisonment for debt. Both Covenants start with an Article that reads:

> All peoples have the right of self-determination. By virtue of that right they freely determine their political status and freely pursue their economic, social and cultural development.

These two Covenants, taken together with the Universal Declaration, are sometimes referred to as the 'International Bill of Rights'.

The ideological and political struggle between the superpowers dominated the international human rights agenda during the 1950s, and the initial post-war momentum that led to the adoption of the Universal Declaration diminished considerably. However, the human rights impetus at the United Nations gained momentum again in the early 1960s, primarily as a result of decolonization. Most of the African and Asian countries that had been under colonial rule when the UN was founded were now becoming independent. Many of these states had a particular interest in human rights issues as a result of their colonial history. UN membership quickly doubled and, by the mid-1960s, developing countries became the largest voting bloc in the General Assembly. The participation of these states stimulated the human rights activities of the UN and took the international human rights agenda in new directions.

Other human rights treaties adopted at the United Nations

In addition to the so-called 'International Bill of Human Rights', the UN system is the source of a number of other international human rights instruments. The other treaties that are considered 'core' to the human rights system include the *International Convention on the Elimination of All Forms of Racial Discrimination*, which came into force in 1969 and prohibits:

> any distinction, exclusion, restriction or preference based on race, colour, descent, or national or ethnic origin which has the purpose or effect of nullifying or impairing the recognition, enjoyment or exercise, on an equal footing, of human rights and fundamental freedoms in the political, economic, social, cultural or any other field of public life.

The *Convention on the Elimination of All Forms of Discrimination against Women* is designed to ensure women have equal access to political and public life as well as education, health, and employment. Under this Convention, which entered into force in 1981, states are also obliged:

> To modify the social and cultural patterns of conduct of men and women, with a view to achieving the elimination of prejudices and customary and all other practices which are based on the idea of the inferiority or the superiority of either of the sexes or on stereotyped roles for men and women.

The *Convention against Torture and Other Cruel, Inhuman or Degrading Treatment or Punishment* came into force in 1987. The Convention includes a definition of torture (for the purposes of the Convention), and insists that any party to it undertakes obligations: to take measures to prevent acts of torture in any territory under its jurisdiction; not to return any person to a state where there are substantial grounds for believing that that person would be in danger of being subjected to torture; and to ensure that acts of torture can be prosecuted in the courts of that state even though those acts occurred abroad. We examine the prohibition on torture and other inhuman and degrading treatment in the next chapter.

The *Convention on the Rights of the Child* defines a child as 'every human being below the age of eighteen unless under the law applicable to the child, majority is attained earlier'. It seeks to protect children from practices that particularly endanger their welfare, including economic exploitation, trafficking, illicit use of drugs, and all forms of sexual exploitation and abuse. The guiding principles of the Convention are the need to take into account the child's best interests, non-discrimination, and respect for the wishes of the child. The Convention entered into force in 1990 and has become the most widely ratified of all UN human rights treaties. The only UN member states not to have ratified the Convention are Somalia and the United States.

The seventh core human rights treaty is the *International Convention on the Protection of the Rights of All Migrant Workers and their Families*, which entered into force in 2003. Unfortunately, the states that have accepted obligations under this treaty are mostly states that *export* migrant workers rather than those that host them. This diminishes the effectiveness and scope of the treaty obligations and means that those states that host migrant workers avoid the reach of this treaty and the prospect of supervision by the monitoring body.

Two new treaties were adopted at the end of 2006. The first is the *International Convention on the Rights of Persons with Disabilities*. Key rights concern the right to make decisions, the right to marry, the right to have a family, the right to work, and the right to education. States are obliged to refrain from discrimination on grounds of disability and to take measures to eliminate such discrimination by 'any person, organization or private enterprise'. The second treaty is the *International Convention for the Protection of All Persons from Enforced Disappearance*. It establishes the prospect of national prosecutions and extraditions for the crime of enforced disappearance. This crime is defined as:

> the arrest, detention, abduction or any other form of deprivation of
> liberty committed by agents of the State or by persons or groups
> of persons acting with the authorization, support or acquiescence of
> the State, followed by a refusal to acknowledge the deprivation
> of liberty or by concealment of the fate or whereabouts of the
> disappeared person, which place such a person outside the
> protection of the law.

Protecting human rights through the treaties

These treaties, and a series of parallel developments at the regional levels of the Organization of American States, the Council of Europe, and the African Union, articulate a range of rights and testify to governments' stated desire to protect human rights. But do they work? Clearly the daily evidence of human rights violations suggests that drafting and signing treaties is not enough. Considerable effort has been expended to make the treaty guarantees more effective. This has been undertaken on a number of fronts.

First, expert monitoring bodies have been established to examine the reports of governments on how they fulfil their human rights obligations. This involves a 'constructive dialogue' over two or three days and results in 'concluding observations' from the relevant committee. Some monitoring bodies engage in fact-finding and country visits. In the context of the prevention of torture, the Council of Europe's expert body makes periodic and *ad hoc* visits to places of detention in 46 European states. A new UN committee will undertake similar visits to those states that ratify a new treaty.

Second, under some treaties, complaints can be brought by aggrieved individuals against the state at the international level (usually only against those states that specifically recognize a 'right to complain' under the treaty). In particular, one has to recognize the remarkable work of the regional bodies such as the European and American Courts of Human Rights and the African Commission on Human and Peoples' Rights. These bodies have developed an impressive case-law which not only develops our understanding of the scope of human rights, but has led to some concrete protection and changes in the law. This system for individual complaints is at the same time remarkable for the volume of judgments delivered in Europe (the European Court of Human Rights delivered over 1,000 judgments in

2005) and for its astonishing under-utilization in the rest of the world (for example, in a similar period the UN Human Rights Committee published its views on the merits of 27 individual communications).

Third, consolidation of these rights in treaties can empower victims to remind the authorities of their international obligations, and this in turn legitimizes a whole series of demands and protests, whether through judicial or other processes at the national level.

Finally, in some cases, such as genocide, torture, and enforced disappearances, the treaties establish the legal framework for the prosecution of individuals who are caught outside their own country. The torture treaty was used to reject legal arguments that certain individuals enjoy immunity from such prosecutions (this is what happened to Senator Pinochet when he was detained in London).

Relying on these treaties to better human rights protection remains unsatisfactory. The monitoring of governments' compliance with their treaty obligations largely depends on self-reporting and 'shadow reporting' by civil society. The monitoring bodies (comprised of independent experts) do an admirable job of analysing the human rights situation in a country and recommending the steps a government needs to take to bring itself into compliance with its human rights obligations. But, in the context of a state's stubborn refusal to cooperate, the monitoring bodies have only the power of publicity. Publicity is only effective to the extent that others report and care about the exposed shortcomings of the government in question.

It is hard to test the actual impact of these treaties. The translation of the principles is subtle and takes effect over time. We will never know all the human rights violations that were actually avoided due to officials thinking twice before taking action. There is, however, concrete evidence of improvements having been made as a result of recommendations contained in the reports of the monitoring bodies. In some cases, national policies have been rethought to bring them into compliance with human rights principles, and in other cases, individual complaints have given rise to radical changes in law and practice. Concrete examples of such changes can be found in the follow-up to judgments of the European Court of Human Rights interpreting and applying the European Convention on Human Rights. One could cite the following as well known examples of the United Kingdom changing its laws as a result of cases brought before the European Court of Human Rights: the ban on interrogation techniques being used against suspected terrorists (wall-standing, hooding, sleep deprivation, and the use of white noise); the decriminalization of sexual activity between men in Northern Ireland; the abolition of corporal punishment in all schools; the development of a statutory scheme for telephone tapping; the prevention of deportations to countries where the deportee would be at risk of torture; overturning the ban on gay men and lesbians in the armed forces; and the recognition of the rights of transsexuals, including a right to marry. Since 2000, the UK's Human Rights Act has made it possible to bring complaints of violations of rights contained in this European Convention directly before the national courts.

These are important gains but we ought to return to the bigger picture. The annual human rights reports prepared by groups such as Amnesty International and Human Rights Watch illustrate how the human rights situation in the world remains bleak. Despite the widely accepted regional and international treaties, human rights violations remain in all parts of the world. Perhaps the following passages will provide a flavour of some of the continuing challenges.

Amnesty International concluded in 2005 with regard to Africa that:

Millions of men, women and children remained impoverished and deprived of clean water, adequate housing, food, education and primary health care. This situation was exacerbated by widespread and systemic corruption and the apparent indifference of governments to providing their citizens with the most basic economic and social rights. Across the region, hundreds of thousands of families were forcibly evicted from their homes, further violating their fundamental human rights.

Amnesty's assessment of the Americas in 2005 read as follows:

Members of the security forces continued to commit widespread human rights violations with impunity. Across the region torture and other ill-treatment, sometimes resulting in deaths in custody, were reported but few of the perpetrators were punished. Victims, their relatives or those representing them when they filed complaints, as well as witnesses, members of the judiciary and investigators, were frequently intimidated, harassed, threatened with death and sometimes killed.

In Asia:

Attacks against civilians by armed groups affected many parts of the region, including Afghanistan, Bangladesh, India, Indonesia, Nepal and Sri Lanka. Bombings caused carnage and robbed hundreds of people of their lives. Some state responses to such attacks were disproportionate and at times discriminated against marginal or minority groups, reinforcing pre-existing grievances or persecution.

In the Middle East and North Africa:

With few exceptions, perpetrators of human rights abuses continued to benefit from impunity as governments failed to hold them to account and ensure justice for their victims. In many countries in the region, security and intelligence services were given free rein to detain suspects for long periods, often holding

them incommunicado and without charge and exposing them to
torture and ill-treatment, confident that they did so with official
acquiescence and without fear of intervention by the courts.

And in Europe:

Many countries in the region were a magnet for those attempting
to escape poverty, violence or persecution. The fact that asylum
is principally a human rights issue continued to be all but lost in
the face of political pressure to control 'illegal immigration' or
to prioritize 'security concerns'. In breach of their international
obligations, some states unlawfully detained asylum-seekers and
conducted expulsions without due process, including to countries
where those seeking protection were at further risk of violations.
Asylum-seekers, migrants and minorities remained among those
continuing to face racism and discrimination across the
region.

All the governments referred to in the detailed country reports
are bound by international human rights law. To place our faith
in treaties and declarations seems rather foolish. But rather than
dismissing the treaties discussed in this section as a distraction or
inadequate for the task, it is perhaps preferable to see the treaties
as providing the framework against which we can legitimately
judge the performance of governments. In the absence of the
Universal Declaration, the human rights treaties, and the
subsequent translation of these texts into national law, it would be
too easy to dismiss the notion of human rights as nonsense or an
imposition of foreign values.

Chapter 3
Human rights foreign policy and the role of the United Nations

The story of the UN's human rights treaties may leave us dissatisfied. Where is the enforcement of these rights? We have a legal framework and reports from non-governmental organizations, but where is the pressure to ensure that these rights are realized in practice? What does it really mean when governments say that their foreign policy is concerned with promoting and protecting human rights? Only very rarely do governments actually use these treaties to bring international complaints against other states. Human rights in foreign policy deserve some exposition.

The idea that governments can legitimately concern themselves with the way in which another state treats its own nationals is a relatively recent innovation in international relations. The concept of non-interference in domestic affairs loomed large for much of the 20th century and was seen to foreclose meaningful human rights foreign policy (see Box 11).

By the time of the 50th anniversary of the Universal Declaration of Human Rights in 1998, it was becoming commonplace to raise human rights issues in foreign relations, but many of those concerned with *realpolitik* saw the exchanges as little more than cosmetic. Interviewed for the anniversary, Alan Clarke, the

> **Box 11: Preface to *The Lawful Rights of Mankind* by Paul Sieghart**
>
> Down to the end of the second world war, it was a matter of universally accepted doctrine in international affairs that how a state treated its own citizens was a matter entirely for its own sovereign determination, and not the legitimate concern of anyone outside its own frontiers. Had a well-meaning delegation from abroad called on Chancellor Adolf Hitler in 1936 to complain about the notorious Nürnberg laws, and the manner in which they were being applied to persecute German Jews, the Führer would probably have dismissed such an initiative with the classic phrase of 'an illegitimate interference in the internal affairs of the sovereign German state', pointing out that these laws had been enacted in full accordance with the provisions of the German Constitution, by an assembly constitutionally and legally competent to enact them, and that neither they nor their application were the concern of meddling foreigners. And in international law as it then stood, he would have been perfectly right – and so would party Secretary-General Josef Stalin have been if a similar delegation had called upon him at around the same time to complain about the wholesale destruction of the kulaks in the Soviet Union.

former British Defence Minister, saw the clash of interests in the following terms:

> My principal duty is to the people of my own country. Diplomacy is a matter of reconciling, either by compromise or threat, conflicting national interests, and the considerations about the Universal Declaration of Human Rights come fairly low on the list of priorities.

Such an approach has nearly always governed international relations and is still prevalent in parts of important foreign ministries, but the significant point is that perceptions about what are the actual 'national interests' can change. Governments are increasingly susceptible to the idea that the nation wants issues of human rights raised with other governments in meaningful ways, and that improving human rights abroad may indeed be in the national interest: as security threats diminish, international stability increases. In addition, we can idealistically hope that the national interest includes the idea that millions of nationals are actually altruistic, rather than selfish, and are concerned about remedying the suffering of others, wherever they may be.

Many national governments have more recently established human rights units within their foreign offices, advisory committees on human rights, and even ministers for human rights. As the legal framework develops, and as rhetoric gives way to constructive discussion, more and more governments may come to see human rights policy and expertise as something central to all aspects of government and foreign relations. Of course, there is a difference between proclaiming that human rights are at the heart of foreign policy, and actually changing the way decisions are taken. Respect for human rights may now be said to be a factor to be considered in a number of spheres of inter-state decision making: admission to certain international and regional organizations; trade agreements and preferential tariffs; export credit guarantees; arms transfers; foreign direct investment; cooperation with international financial institutions; UN technical assistance programmes; development work; international investment agreements; customs communities; and the maintenance of international peace and security. The human rights record or reputation of a state can adversely affect any of the above. A willingness to improve human rights has also almost become a condition for entering into a range of diverse arrangements with other states. One obvious example is that respect for human rights has become a formal pre-condition for admission to the European Union. In short, all states, through their representatives, now care about how their human rights record is regarded internationally. In contrast to this apparent progress, we must remind ourselves that promoting human rights in other countries still comes pretty low down the list of priorities when there is a perceived clash with other competing 'national interests'. The extent to which this will change depends on the enthusiasm of people to hold their leaders to a human rights foreign policy that reorganizes these priorities.

The limits of human rights foreign policy

The promotion of human rights through foreign policy may be open to criticism on several grounds. First, there is the reaction from certain states which see a creeping justification for the use of military force. There was a sharp reaction from key states to the NATO bombing of Serbia (in connection with Kosovo). The speech of the Chinese Ambassador to the United Nations in Geneva illustrates the suspicion which human rights foreign policy can arouse in states.

> Recently, some people turn upside down the relationship between sovereignty and human rights in an attempt to impose with force their human rights values on others, and even with this excuse pursue a hegomistic policy and legalize their aggression activities. If this policy is stubbornly pursued, not only protection of human rights could not be genuinely guaranteed, but even global peace and security will be under threat.

President Yeltsin of Russia rebuked the United States with regard to the NATO bombing in similar terms, rejecting the human rights justification:

> ... not all of the ideas which have surfaced in the course of discussions about the future of Europe strike us as being well-founded. I have in mind the calls for 'humanitarian intervention' – a new idea – in the internal affairs of another State, even when they are made under the pretext of defending human rights and freedoms. We all know what disproportionate consequences such intervention can have.

> It is sufficient to recall NATO's aggression, spearheaded by the
> United States of America, against Yugoslavia.

This suspicion that claims about human rights violations are being used as a pretext to justify military intervention has not gone away since the Kosovo intervention in 1999. In fact, there has been a greater conceptualization of the connection between human rights violations and military intervention. The developing recognition of the need to repress and prevent international crimes, such as genocide and other crimes against humanity, has been linked to the developing possibility of a right for states to intervene militarily in another state on humanitarian grounds (so-called 'humanitarian intervention'). Following the disagreement in the UN Security Council over the 1999 NATO intervention to protect the population of Kosovo, various governments, including that of the United Kingdom, sought to outline situations in which it would be legal for states to use force against another state in the face of a 'humanitarian catastrophe' (see Box 12).

Box 12: UK Foreign Secretary Robin Cook, January 2000

The UK submitted to the UN Secretary-General: 'a set of ideas to help the international community decide when it is right to act.

- first, any intervention is by definition a failure of prevention. Force should always be the last resort;

- second, the immediate responsibility for halting violence rests with the state in which it occurs;

- but, third, when faced with an overwhelming humanitarian catastrophe and a government that has demonstrated itself unwilling or unable to halt or prevent it, the international community should act;

- and finally, any use of force in this context should be collective, proportionate, likely to achieve its objective, and carried out in accordance with international law.'

The International Commission on Intervention and State Sovereignty reoriented the popular notion of 'humanitarian intervention' into a *responsibility to protect*. The idea of the 'responsibility to protect' was presented by the Commission as being derived from a need to avoid a perceived militarization of humanitarian work and to avoid prejudging the motives for intervention by simply labelling them 'humanitarian'. There was a desire to force a reconceptualization of the issues. Heads of State and Government, meeting at the UN's 2005 Summit, endorsed this new concept and declared themselves ready to take timely decisive collective action when states are manifestly failing to protect their populations from 'genocide, war crimes, ethnic cleansing and crimes against humanity'. While a strict reading of the text does not alter the need for the approval of the UN Security Council before military force is used, the developments in this field raise the possibility for states to feel more comfortable using military force against another state in response to the latter's failure to protect its people. Already the states of the African Union have agreed that a founding principle of the Union is: 'The right of the Union to intervene in a Member State pursuant to a decision of the Assembly in respect of grave circumstances, namely war crimes, genocide and crimes against humanity.' Calls for force to be used to protect the civilian population in the contexts of Rwanda, Srebrenica, Kosovo, and Darfur have built on the concepts of crimes against humanity and war crimes to justify the use of military action. We can say that, in light of the recent failure of the international community to protect the people of Bosnia and Rwanda, there is a greater expectation that effective protection will be offered in the face of ongoing genocide or crimes against humanity. The concern with regard to the atrocities in Darfur constantly recalls this global commitment. However, the protection offered to the people of Darfur has remained tragically inadequate, as the rapes and killings continued through 2006. The grand principle of the responsibility to protect looks rather hollow from the perspective of today's victims of armed conflict.

An assessment of human rights-based justifications for the use of military force is complicated by the following factors. First, in many situations there will be a danger that the necessary force used to intervene could do more harm than good. People get killed in military interventions; how many deaths are justified to save more lives? Even where human rights violations are actually ongoing, human rights activists have sometimes baulked at supporting the use of military force in the name of human rights. The US-based organization Human Rights Watch wrote in its 2004 *World Report*:

> now that the war's proponents are relying so significantly on a humanitarian rationale for the war, the need to assess this claim has grown in importance. We conclude that, despite the horrors of Saddam Hussein's rule, the invasion of Iraq cannot be justified as a humanitarian intervention.

By contrast, others have justified the war against Iraq on the basis that it brought about the downfall of the Saddam Hussein regime and ushered in freedom and democracy for the people of Iraq. Evidently, the fight for human rights has become entangled with controversial justifications for the use of massive military force. The issue cannot easily be resolved, as there may well be cases where force must be used to protect people from immediate violence. As human rights organizations enter the terrain of endorsing and protesting the use of military intervention, determining at what point force should be used, and who should use it, is one of the biggest challenges facing the human rights movement.

A second strand of opposition sees Western human rights foreign policy as disguising hegemonic ambitions and rejects human rights as incompatible with so-called 'Asian values'. Part of the Asian values reaction is a simple rejection of Western interference in the political affairs of certain countries in the Far East. But another part comes from a sense that the Western notion of

6. 'No war in the name of human rights': A demonstration in Berne (Switzerland) against the 2003 Iraq war

human rights has paid too little attention to the correlative responsibilities which ought to accompany the exercise of human rights. Yash Ghai has sought to explain why the end of the Cold War led to this backlash against the renewed enthusiasm for human rights foreign policy:

The emphasis on rights was not welcomed by all States ... Those States which had felt immune from international scrutiny of their authoritarian political systems (which in East and South East Asia had been justified on the basis of the menace of communism) found themselves a little like the emperor without clothes. They were anxious at what were considered to be the likely consequences of this new stress on human rights for their political systems. They were also resentful of conditionalities that derogated from their political and economic sovereignty. The universalization of rights was seen as the imposition of Western norms. They were anxious because of the effects of these rights on their competitiveness in the framework of international trade that was ushered in by globalization, and they claimed to detect in this emphasis a Western conspiracy to undermine newly growing economics.

In fact, the reaction may be understood as the position of a few government representatives and internationally recognized elites, rather than the cultural specificity of a whole continent.

Amartya Sen tackles the currency given to the 'Asian values' assault on human rights and argues that voices have 'persistently been raised in favour of freedom – in different forms – in distinct and distant cultures'. He concludes his chapter on 'Culture and Human Rights':

> As far as the authoritarian claims about 'Asian values' are concerned, it has to be recognized that values that have been championed in the past in Asian countries – in east Asia as well as elsewhere in Asia – include an enormous variety. Indeed, in many ways they are similar to substantial variations that are often seen in the history of ideas in the West also. To see Asian history in terms of a narrow category of authoritarian values does little justice to the rich varieties of thought in Asian intellectual traditions. Dubious history does nothing to vindicate dubious politics.

This debate has lost much of its sting. Respect for others, the protection of human dignity, equality, self-determination, and tolerance of others' beliefs can arguably be discerned in many cultures, traditions, and religions. As we have already suggested, the reality is that the correct balance between the liberty of the individual and the needs of the community will vary depending on the context. Such an admission is not a negation of the idea of 'universal' human rights. The same fundamental human rights exist everywhere – but concrete questions regarding respect for individual rights in individual cases will yield different answers depending on the context. Even when a tribunal can conclude that different national considerations need to be taken into account in deciding whether a state has correctly balanced a right against the needs of the community, the values that underpin the importance of respect for these rights remain universally accepted. Briefly stated, the underlying idea that the dignity or moral worth of a person should be respected can be found in the values adopted by various peoples, religions, and civilizations.

We might add that in the 21st century, resistance to the human rights message is not confined to an Asian/Western clash. Some formerly socialist countries have sometimes shown little enthusiasm for the economic, social, and cultural rights that were, for so long, part of their foreign policy attack on the West. Now, as emerging economies, they perceive attempts to impose welfare state-like regulation as possible impediments to economic development. It is also fair to say that there is antagonism from some people in such transitional economies towards 'state law' and 'state regulations'. This is not an Asian or Eastern European phenomenon but is based on opinions as to the potential market benefits that are perceived to flow from minimal regulation in the economic sphere, and a sense of disadvantage believed to follow from compliance with internationally recognized labour standards. In these situations, the suspicion is that human rights are being used to achieve economic dominance (rather than hegemonic control through military or cultural means) by holding back the development of fragile economies in transition.

In particular, the idea of a 'social clause' (which allows a state to impose trade sanctions on states that fail to respect core labour standards) has been treated with suspicion. The incorporation of such a clause into the multilateral trading rules of the World Trade Organization (WTO) has been rejected by developing countries. Several governments in a position to support trade sanctions, such as the United Kingdom, have declared their opposition to the use of such sanctions to enforce full compliance with all labour standards, on the grounds that such trade sanctions 'punish countries for their poverty, and hurt the poorest most'.

Third, a human rights foreign policy may suggest that promoting human rights is about changing what *other* governments do, rather than examining respect for these rights at home. Foreign ministries are unlikely to turn their attention to domestic human rights violations. For example, the US Department of State's *Country Reports on Human Rights Practices* does not cover the human rights situation in the United States. The Assistant Secretary of State explained at the launch of the 2005 report:

> The 196 reports include every member country of the UN, except of course the United States. We do however consider the human rights performance of any government, including our own, to be a legitimate subject for international comment and debate.

Human rights foreign policy is always skewed towards the 'other'. For some time this really was a one-way street. Today, not only is there a preparedness on the part of some governments to publicly criticize another government's human rights record, but we now see that a target government is often ready to turn the tables. Consider the following exchange between the United States and China at the UN Commission on Human Rights in 2000:

The US Secretary of State, Madeleine Albright, arguing for a resolution expressing concern over the human rights situation in China, presented her case as follows:

> [China] has signed the International Covenant on Civil and Political Rights. Unfortunately, its official policies have always fallen well short of these standards, and deteriorated markedly this past year.
>
> During that period, there were widespread arrests of those seeking to exercise their right to peaceful political expression. Thousands of members of the Falun Gong movement were detained. Authorities continued to limit the ability of Christians, Muslims, and Buddhists to worship in accordance with custom and conscience. Minority groups such as the Tibetans and Uighurs were barred from fully exercising their cultural and linguistic heritage.

Qiao Zonghuai, the Chinese Ambassador, robustly exercised his 'right of reply':

> The United States is used to pointing fingers at other countries' human rights situation, but back in its own country, there exist gross violations of human rights: notorious racial discrimination, police brutality, torture in prison, infringement on women's rights and campus gun killings. A country like the US with such poor human rights record has no right to judge other countries' human rights situation at UN forum. We advise that, instead of interfering in the internal affairs of other countries under the pretext of human rights, the US should spend more time to examine its own human rights situation. Otherwise it will end up with lifting a rock only to drop it on his own feet.

This is not an exchange about 'Asian values'. This is about seeing that human rights foreign policy is only convincing when rooted in respect for the same values at home. Joseph Nye's recent appeal for the use of 'soft power' recognizes this challenge:

The United States, like other countries, expresses its values in what it does and what it says. Political values like democracy and human rights can be powerful sources of attraction, but it is not just enough to proclaim them. ... Others watch how Americans implement our values at home as well as abroad. A Swedish diplomat recently told me, 'All countries want to promote the values we believe in. I think the most criticized part of the US's (and possibly most rich countries') soft power 'packaging' is the perceived double standard and inconsistencies.' Perceived hypocrisy is particularly corrosive of power that is based on proclaimed values. Those who scorn or despise us for hypocrisy are less likely to want to help us achieve our policy objectives.

Fourth, governments do not promote all rights in all places. Different governments have different priorities. The United States, for instance, has failed to embrace economic and social rights or the right to development. The United States treats the promotion of the rights of the child as liable to conflict with established parental rights in US law, and it obviously takes a back seat with regard to concerns about the death penalty. The 2005 US State Department's report explains:

> The Country Reports on Human Rights Practices cover internationally recognized individual, civil, political and worker rights, as set forth in the Universal Declaration of Human Rights. These rights include freedom from torture or other cruel, inhuman or degrading treatment or punishment, from prolonged detention without charges, from disappearance or clandestine detention, and from other flagrant violations of the right to life, liberty and the security of the person.

(See Box 13 for an example of a Country Report.) Such country reports are often criticized for bias or spin. We should perhaps not be surprised that there are differences of opinion on how one government should present the situation in another country. Despite the limited list of rights and the prospect of lack of

Box 13: US Department of State Country Report 2005: Sudan

The government's human rights record remained poor, and there were numerous serious problems, including evidence of continuing genocide in Darfur, for which the government and *janjaweed* continued to bear responsibility. The following human rights problems were reported:

- abridgement of citizens' rights to change their government
- evidence of war crimes
- extrajudicial and other unlawful killings by members of the security forces and government-allied militias acting with impunity
- killings of civilians in conflict
- abductions
- torture, beatings, and rape by security forces
- harsh and life-threatening prison conditions
- arbitrary arrest and detention, including incommunicado detention of suspected government opponents, and prolonged pretrial detention
- executive interference in the judiciary and denial of fair trial in civilian and military courts
- forced military conscription of underage men
- obstructions to humanitarian assistance in Darfur
- infringement of citizens' privacy rights
- severe restrictions on freedom of speech, press, assembly, association, religion, and movement within the country
- harassment and detention of internally displaced persons (IDPs)
- harassment of human rights organizations

- **violence and discrimination against women and female genital mutilation (FGM)**
- **abuse of children, particularly in Darfur**
- **trafficking in persons**
- **discrimination and violence against ethnic minorities**
- **denial of workers' rights**
- **forced labor, including forced child labor, by security forces and associated militias**
- **widespread child labor**

objectivity, these reports remain influential for decision making in the context of trade preferences, foreign investment, loans, development, and military assistance.

We can compare the European Union's Common Foreign and Security Policy on human rights. Although there is an *EU Annual Report on Human Rights*, this does not offer country profiles but rather describes the initiatives taken over the year by the EU. The 2005 report is clear that EU policy is not confined to civil, political, and workers' rights:

> The European Union attaches the same importance to economic, social and cultural rights as to civil and political rights, bearing in mind the universality, indivisibility, interdependence and inter-relatedness of all human rights and fundamental freedoms, as confirmed by the 1993 World Conference on Human Rights, held in Vienna. Both categories of rights stem from the inherent dignity of the human person and the effective implementation of each right is indispensable for the full implementation of others.

Furthermore, a look at the sorts of human rights projects that were funded in 2004 reveals a particular set of priorities. The European Initiative for Democracy and Human Rights had resources amounting to more than 100 million Euros, funding projects in 32 countries, with the following priority areas:

> the promotion of democracy, the rule of law and good governance, abolition of the death penalty, combating torture and impunity, support for the international criminal tribunals and the International Criminal Court, combating racism and xenophobia and discrimination against minorities, as well as the protection of the rights of indigenous peoples.

The extent to which the human rights record of a country is actually raised in international relations still depends on the willingness of governments seriously to raise such issues. Enthusiasm for human rights in foreign policy ebbs and flows. Different governments and different ministers make different promises. In 1998, UK Foreign Secretary Robin Cook stated:

> I am instructing our posts around the world to report regularly on the use of torture in the countries they cover, to raise individual cases with their host governments, and to maintain contact with the medical, legal and human rights groups tackling the problem. That way we can ensure that our efforts have the biggest possible impact.

Raising individual cases with governments can be effective, although the nature of such quiet diplomacy makes it difficult to evaluate. But the promise that it is done takes us into a new era of human rights foreign policy. Switzerland has gone so far as to enshrine in its Constitution a foreign policy commitment to contribute to the alleviation of need and poverty in the world as well as to the promotion of respect for human rights and democracy. According the Department of Foreign Affairs, Swiss Federal Councillors 'address human rights questions with their foreign counterparts when visiting them in their own countries'.

Raising human rights through diplomatic channels can sometimes lead to concrete results, but such *démarches* are usually of little use without the threat of some sanction or positive incentive. The former EU Commissioner Chris Patten has written of his frustration at the hours of wasted time spent negotiating human rights clauses in agreements that he knew would never be activated against violating states. In Patten's words: 'Winking at electrodes, as it were, makes for wretched diplomacy. Few authoritarian governments go weak at the knees at the prospect of a European *démarche*.'

In a way, all states have a human rights foreign policy to the extent that they participate in the human rights debates and initiatives at the United Nations, and it is to this subject that we now turn.

UN action on human rights

Early on, the UN established a Commission on Human Rights initially composed of nine core individual members. These individuals proposed that Commission members should act as independent experts rather than present the views of their governments. The governments themselves rejected this proposal. The UN member states decided that the Commission should comprise governmental representatives from 18 elected UN member states. This membership of government representatives was expanded to 32 in 1967, and later to 53 members. In 2006, the Commission was abolished and replaced with a 47-member Human Rights Council.

Before examining the new Council, we might pause to consider what the Commission achieved during its 60-year history. The Commission's agenda has fluctuated over the years, responding to the shifting balance of power between its member governments. The first years of the Commission's work focused on standard setting, which it accomplished through the drafting of the Universal Declaration and the International Covenants. With the arrival of members from the developing world in the 1960s, issues of racial discrimination in Southern Africa and the Israeli

7. The Mothers of the Plaza de Mayo, who gathered weekly at the Plaza de Mayo in Buenos Aires to demand justice for their children who 'disappeared' during the Argentine military dictatorship between 1976 and 1983

occupation came to the forefront of the Commission's agenda. Following concern over the 1973 coup in Chile against the Socialist Government of President Allende and the associated human rights violations in Chile and in Argentina, the Commission's agenda adapted in the 1980s to include public and confidential discussion of such country situations.

The Commission developed a series of 'special procedures' for monitoring violations in selected countries, through individuals acting either as country or thematic experts. These experts submit reports to the relevant UN bodies. They undertake country visits which are the subject of separate reports, and, in addition, they correspond with governments through 'urgent appeals' and 'letters of allegation'. These 'communications' allege human rights violations and generate some responses from governments. (In 2005, the response rate was 46%.) Even where the faxes and letters are ignored or dismissed, it is clear that the process of putting governments on notice that the UN's watchdogs have been alerted has led to releases and changes in policy. By any account, the work of these *pro-bono* human rights experts provides a remarkable tapestry of human rights information, analysis, and recommendations. (See Box 14 for lists of the countries and themes covered so far.)

Box 14: Situations subjected to UN special procedures

Afghanistan, Belarus, Bolivia, Burundi, Cambodia, Chad, Chile, Cuba, Democratic People's Republic of Korea, Democratic Republic of the Congo/Zaire, El Salvador, Equatorial Guinea, former Yugoslavia, Guatemala, Haiti, Iran, Iraq, Liberia, Myanmar, Nigeria, Occupied Kuwait, Palestinian territories occupied since 1967, Poland, Romania, Rwanda, Somalia, Sudan, and Uzbekistan.

Thematic expert mechanisms in order of their creation

Enforced or involuntary disappearances; extrajudicial, summary or arbitrary executions; torture and other cruel, inhuman or degrading treatment or punishment; freedom of religion or belief; mercenaries; sale of children, child prostitution and child pornography; arbitrary detention; internally displaced; racism and xenophobia; freedom of expression; right to development; violence against women; independence of judges and lawyers; structural adjustment policies and foreign debt; toxic and dangerous products and wastes; right to education; children in armed conflict; restitution, compensation and rehabilitation for victims; extreme poverty; migrants; right to food; adequate housing; human rights defenders; indigenous peoples; right to health; racial discrimination faced by people of African descent; human rights and counter-terrorism; minority issues; international solidarity; trafficking in persons; human rights and transnational corporations and other business enterprises.

Why was the Commission abolished? The perception started to grow in 2001 that a bloc of states was shielding themselves and their allies from being condemned by the 53-member body. It was alleged that governments were seeking election to the Commission in order to table procedural motions and swap votes to insulate themselves from condemnation (see Box 15). This perception lay behind the campaign to reform the elections process to the Commission. The result was the new Human Rights Council. The Commission itself, while providing a forum for such reporting, had come to be seen in some quarters as a place where governments banded together to prevent collective condemnation of their own records. The criticism of the Commission was not only related to the image of some members of the Commission but also to the Commission's collective failure to act in certain situations. On the one hand, the head of the US delegation, Jeane Kirkpatrick, complained in 2003 that no resolution had been passed 'condemning repression in Chechnya, or slavery and repression in Sudan, or murder and violation of rights in Zimbabwe, or the continued victimization of the Falun Gong in China'. On the other hand, several observers, such as Human Rights Watch, drew attention to the failure of the Commission, not only over situations such as those in Zimbabwe and China, but also over the resistance by the United States and the EU to

Box 15: Ken Roth, Human Rights Watch, April 2001

The latest batch of new members illustrates how poorly this system works. They include such dubious paragons of human rights virtue as Algeria, the Democratic Republic of the Congo, Kenya, Libya, Saudi Arabia, Syria and Vietnam. Needless to say, such governments do not seek membership out of a commitment to promote human rights abroad or to improve their own abysmal human rights records. Rather they join the commission to protect themselves from criticism and to undermine its work.

allow the Commission to consider properly the invasion and occupation of Iraq and the human rights situation in Afghanistan. The criticism was that the UN body had become selective in its examination and that the selection was being operated by the same governments that ought to be condemned. Commentators repeatedly pointed out, in what became a cliché, that the foxes were guarding the chicken coup.

The resulting reform was centred on making the election process for membership of the human rights body more difficult. In 2006, the 191 UN member states elected by majority, and in a secret ballot, the founding members of the new Human Rights Council.

Two features of the new Human Rights Council are worth mentioning here. First, by sitting throughout the year in short blocks for no less than ten weeks (rather than in one six-week block), it is hoped that there can be more sustained scrutiny of situations. Second, a new procedure called 'universal periodic review' is to be implemented in 2007, in which the Council will review every UN member state's compliance with its human rights obligations and commitments. The theory is that this procedure will avoid the Commission's previous selectivity by examining every state in the world with respect to the full range of its human rights obligations. The Council's founding document provides that it will be responsible for 'promoting universal respect for the protection of all human rights and fundamental freedoms for all'. In other words, universal periodic review will look at all rights in all countries.

It is perhaps too early to say whether these new arrangements will lead to a more satisfying set of condemnations. As was suggested above, it is perhaps a vain hope to expect governments to act as objective human rights evaluators. Human rights foreign policy, at the UN or elsewhere, will always be about balancing concern for human rights with other competing interests.

The media tends to focus on the output of UN bodies such as the Commission, and now the Council; but to concentrate on the behaviour of diplomats at the United Nations is to overlook much of the UN's activity on human rights. In addition to the UN's monitoring of states through the expert treaty bodies (discussed in Chapter 2) and the special procedures (discussed above), the UN has expanded its attention to human rights in further important contexts. First, a number of UN field operations have been established with a human rights mandate to offer protection, monitor the situation, and offer assistance (most notably in Cambodia, El Salvador, Guatemala, Haiti, Rwanda, Burundi, Sierra Leone, Liberia, Sudan, Democratic Republic of Congo, Colombia, and Nepal). These operations have enjoyed some success in implementing human rights protection and achieving improvements on the ground. Second, the UN programmes and funds that deal with issues such as children, women, health, and development have started to use human rights principles to underpin their work.

Occasionally, the UN is even able to go beyond what the member states have explicitly agreed to do and say. We can detect here a sort of 'supranational' approach to human rights. The UN Secretary-General, the UN High Commissioner for Human Rights, the Human Rights Commissioner for the Council of Europe, and other senior figures from the secretariats of international and regional organizations can operate in ways that go beyond the simple secretarial fulfilment of an inter-state mandate. They can speak up and speak out when governments are unwilling to do so. Much will depend on the determination of the individuals recruited by the relevant inter-governmental organization.

For example, Mary Robinson, as the UN High Commissioner for Human Rights, issued a statement on Chechnya in 1999 expressing concern about the fact that 'indiscriminate and disproportionate use of force is causing high civilian loss of

8. Mary Robinson, UN High Commissioner for Human Rights, in Afghanistan

life and injuries'. At the inter-state level at that time, no inter-governmental body could summon a majority to raise a similar level of concern or take concrete action.

It is telling that even the United States, which has a stated human rights foreign policy, will at times distinguish its approach from that of the UN High Commissioner for Human Rights. Governments may feel the need to 'pull their punches' in terms of lecturing other countries on how to behave or protesting violations of human rights by the security forces. On a tour of Africa by the US Secretary of State, the *New York Times* reported one member of the party as stating: 'We don't do Mary Robinson.' The report continues 'an allusion to UN High Commissioner for Human Rights, who has no other agenda. In Africa today, the United States has many other interests, including the promotion of stability and security, which often means the use of methods not appreciated by human rights groups.'

The fact that an office such as the Office of the High Commissioner for Human Rights has no strategic military or trade interests means that there is a possibility that issues will be raised when this would otherwise be precluded by foreign policy considerations (even in an inter-governmental forum dedicated to human rights). Of course, the Office of the High Commissioner for Human Rights will feel it has to work within the parameters of what is acceptable to governments or risk losing budget, cooperation, and support. But the Office has created some room to develop its own voice and ought to be expected to articulate concern, even outrage, at human rights violations wherever they occur. In recent years the Office has grown in size and ambition. It now has over 500 personnel at its headquarters in Geneva, and about 500 personnel around the world in field presences in places such as Cambodia, Colombia, and Nepal. There is an attempt to make human rights a central part of the UN's work in these places as well as in larger operations such as the one in Sudan. The focus is on shifting from studies and seminars to in-country capacity-building and reinforcing the rule of law worldwide.

Chapter 4
The international crime of torture

We saw above that some human rights violations give rise to individual criminal responsibility. We have referred to war crimes and set out the definitions of genocide and crimes against humanity. Such crimes have sometimes been prosecuted in international tribunals and, on occasion, at the national level. Another international crime is the crime of torture. The prohibition on torture in the UN Convention against Torture is described in absolute terms. ('No exceptional circumstances whatsoever, whether a state of war or a threat of war, internal political instability or any other public emergency, may be invoked as a justification of torture.') But we know that torture unfortunately goes on around the world. In this short chapter, we will focus on four issues: the definition of torture, the arguments that have been put forward to excuse torture in order to prevent a terrorist attack, the prohibition of the use of evidence gleaned from torture, and the ban on sending someone to a country where there is a strong likelihood of them being tortured. It is suggested we can learn a lot about the foundations of human rights thinking from the exploration of these issues. To better understand the challenges involved, it is worth recalling a little of the history of torture.

The purposes of torture have been various. In some contexts torture was considered a useful way to extract confessions and

9. Guy Fawkes's confession, extracted by torture. His shaky signature can barely be made out at the end of the confession and above the signature of the witnesses

essential proof for a conviction at trial. Although the English common law prohibited torture, an exceptional procedure allowed the king to issue 'torture warrants' through the Star Chamber. One of the most famous individuals subjected to this procedure was Guy Fawkes, caught trying to blow up the Houses of Parliament in 1605. He was then tortured into giving up the names of his accomplices. The judges of the House of Lords in a recent human rights case have reminded us of this episode in English history (see Box 16). This form of investigation became seen as emblematic of the abuse of power by the King, it was therefore abolished, along with the Star Chamber, in 1640. Although the Roman-Canon law tradition in Continental Europe continued to accept confessions extracted by torture as useful elements of proof, this practice was increasingly seen, not only as unreliable, but also as unfair to the innocent.

> **Box 16: Lord Hope in *A v Secretary of State for the Home Department* (2005)**
>
> Four hundred years ago, on 4 November 1605, Guy Fawkes was arrested when he was preparing to blow up the Parliament which was to be opened the next day, together with the King and all the others assembled there. Two days later James I sent orders to the Tower authorising torture to be used to persuade Fawkes to confess and reveal the names of his co-conspirators. His letter stated that 'the gentler tortours' were first to be used on him, and that his torturers were then to proceed to the worst until the information was extracted out of him. On 9 November 1605 he signed his confession with a signature that was barely legible and gave the names of his fellow conspirators. On 27 January 1606 he and seven others were tried before a special commission in Westminster Hall. Signed statements in which they had each confessed to treason were shown to them at the trial, acknowledged by them to be their own and then read to the jury.

In modern times we have seen how brutal regimes considered that torture would remind dissidents and the general population who was in charge – and who was determined to remain in charge. In the 1980s, an anti-torture campaign, led by groups such as Amnesty International, was successful in advocating a set of binding international prohibitions on torture. Torture was already criminalized as a war crime when committed against certain prisoners, and was considered an international crime in the context of genocide and crimes against humanity. But the 1984 *Convention against Torture and Other Cruel, Inhuman or Degrading Treatment or Punishment* criminalized torture even outside these contexts, and prescribed individual criminal responsibility for a single act of torture. As already mentioned, Senator Pinochet's arrest and detention in London resulted

The Economist

MAY 8TH–14TH 2004   www.economist.com

Swing states: a series
PAGE 29

Ariel Sharon's Gaza blow
PAGES 12 AND 45

Brazil's need for investment
PAGE 35

Google's unusual flotation
PAGES 14 AND 69

Resign, Rumsfeld

US$4.95 • C$6.95

10. Images of the abuse and humiliation of Iraqi prisoners were
flashed around the world. The photo of the hooded man on a box
with electrical wires became emblematic of the human rights abuses
committed against prisoners in Iraq

from the application of the rules contained in this Convention
and, more recently, we have seen this treaty provide the context
for the arrest in Senegal of the former President of Chad, Hissène
Habré, with a view to his eventual prosecution for crimes of

torture. In 2005, the Afghan rebel leader, Faryadi Zardad, was convicted at the Old Bailey in London of torture and hostage-taking and sentenced to 20 years imprisonment. This represented a rare, but concrete, implementation of the torture treaty.

Let us now see how the absolute prohibition of torture has come under strain in recent times. First, in the wake of the shocking 2001 September 11 attacks on the United States, there were attempts to define torture in a particularly narrow way. The interpretation of the term in a 2002 memorandum of the US Justice Department read torture so narrowly as to amount to the intentional infliction of 'excruciating' or 'agonizing' pain. This looked particularly unfortunate as the photos of the abused Iraqi prisoners surfaced with graphic evidence of the humiliation being meted out. Many blamed the policy makers as well as the disgraced prison guards.

By December 2004, the US Justice Department had replaced the previous memorandum with a public document setting out the US policy and abandoning the idea of such an explicit threshold. Instead, the memorandum details those cases of foreign abuse that had been determined as torture by judicial decisions in the United States. These cases were suits brought against foreign torturers from the Philippines, Iraq, and Iran (see Box 17).

Box 17: From the US Department of Justice memorandum, 2004

Cases in which courts have found torture suggest the nature of the extreme conduct that falls within the statutory definition. *See, e.g., Hilao v Estate of Marcos,* [1996] ... (concluding that a course of conduct that included, among other things, severe beatings of plaintiff, repeated threats of death and electric shock, sleep deprivation, extended shackling to a cot (at times with a towel over

---

> his nose and mouth and water poured down his nostrils),
> seven months of confinement in a 'suffocatingly hot' and
> cramped cell, and eight years of solitary or near-solitary
> confinement, constituted torture); *Mehinovic v Vuckovic*,
> [2002]... (concluding that a course of conduct that included,
> among other things, severe beatings to the genitals, head,
> and other parts of the body with metal pipes, brass knuckles,
> batons, a baseball bat, and various other items; removal of
> teeth with pliers; kicking in the face and ribs; breaking of
> bones and ribs and dislocation of fingers; cutting a figure
> into the victim's forehead; hanging the victim and beating
> him; extreme limitations of food and water; and subjection
> to games of 'Russian roulette', constituted torture); *Daliberti
> v Republic of Iraq*, [2001]... (entering default judgment
> against Iraq where plaintiffs alleged, among other things,
> threats of 'physical torture, such as cutting off ... fingers,
> pulling out ... fingernails', and electric shocks to the testicles);
> *Cicippio v Islamic Republic of Iran*, [1998]... (concluding
> that a course of conduct that included frequent beatings,
> pistol whipping, threats of imminent death, electric shocks,
> and attempts to force confessions by playing Russian roulette
> and pulling the trigger at each denial, constituted torture).

Is it really that important to find the threshold at which coercive
interrogation becomes torture? While the international crime
and the corresponding rules on prosecution and extradition
only attach to conduct which satisfies the legal definition of
'torture', we should recall that the Convention also bans 'other
cruel or inhuman or degrading treatment'. The UN Body of
Principles for All Persons in Detention explicitly states that:

> The term 'cruel, inhuman or degrading treatment or punishment'
> should be interpreted so as to extend the widest possible protection
> against abuses, whether physical or mental, including the holding

of a detained or imprisoned person in conditions which deprive
him, temporarily or permanently, of the use of any of his natural
senses, such as sight or hearing, or of his awareness of place and the
passing of time.

As attention shifted in 2006 to the human right not to be
subjected to cruel, inhuman, or degrading treatment, the US
Attorney-General sought to circumscribe that category by
stating there was 'disagreement' whether 'embarrassing or
insulting' someone should come within that prohibition. Such
attempts to define 'how far can you go?' remind us that the
goal of 'breaking the prisoner' still figures as part of the *modus
operandi* for interrogators seeking to play their role in averting
the next terrorist attack. The purpose of coercive treatment is
no longer really to obtain a confession for trial; it being widely
acknowledged that few legal systems would accept that evidence
procured through such methods should be admitted in court.
The purpose is said to be to gather intelligence about the terrorist
network and to prevent future attacks. This brings us to the
philosophical question: might some incidents of torture or
ill-treatment be justified to avert a terrorist attack? (the ticking
bomb scenario).

The argument that the torture of a few individuals (perhaps
with the reintroduction of torture warrants) could save the lives
of many innocents is repeatedly rehearsed (and not only in the
philosophy classroom). Several counter-arguments have been
developed. First, it is said that information produced under
torture is unreliable as the victim will say anything to avoid the
pain. Therefore, torture is more likely to generate false leads than
help any investigation. Second, it is argued that once allowed in
exceptional circumstances, the use of torture will spread, and
we will find ourselves on a 'slippery slope' where mistreatment is
seen as normal, even expected. Third, it is suggested that torture
is wrong because it negates the whole idea that society exists to
ensure that we all respect each other's worth or dignity.

But even after all the arguments for and against have been played out and torture has been officially outlawed, the idea of justifiable torture sneaks back into the contemporary discourse in the form of the suggestion by some that one could admit a possible defence of 'necessity' in the context of a criminal trial of a torturer (this was the view of the Israeli Supreme Court in 1999 when it declared that the General Security Service had no authority to use certain physical interrogation techniques such as shaking). In a similar vein, in the context of a trial for torture, others have chosen to accept as mitigating circumstances the intention to save life through the infliction of torture and consequently imposed a fine rather than imprisonment. (This was the position of the German court in a 2004 judgment concerning the prosecution of police officers who ordered and threatened pain to be inflicted on a suspected kidnapper who refused to reveal the whereabouts of the child he had taken.) (See Box 18 for further details.)

Box 18: From the article 'Bad Torture – Good Torture?' by Florian Jessberger

On 27 September 2002, law student Magnus Gaefgen kidnapped 11-year-old Jakob von Metzler, the son of a senior bank executive, killed him in his apartment and hid the dead body close to a lake near Frankfurt. In accordance with his plan, he forwarded a letter to the boy's family in which he demanded one million Euro in return for the release of the child. Three days after the boy's disappearance, Gaefgen was arrested after being observed picking up the ransom. During his interrogation, the suspect gave evasive or misleading answers concerning his involvement in the abduction and provided no information about the whereabouts or health status of the boy. Finally, the day after the arrest, Frankfurt Police Vice-President, Wolfgang Daschner, who was responsible for the investigation, ordered that pain be inflicted on the suspect, without causing injuries, under medical supervision and subject to prior warning, in order to save the life of the boy. Accordingly, a subordinate police officer told Gaefgen, who was still in police custody, that the police were prepared to inflict pain on him that 'he would never forget' if he continued to withhold information concerning the whereabouts of the boy. Under the influence of this threat, Gaefgen gave full particulars of the whereabouts of the boy. The actual infliction of pain, which in fact had been arranged by fetching a specially trained police officer, was not necessary. Shortly thereafter, police officers found the body of the boy. ...

The judgment concluded that the act was neither justified nor excused, and that both defendants were criminally responsible.

However, the Court found 'massive mitigating circumstances' in favour of both defendants. The judgment referred in particular to the defendants' aim of saving the life of the child, but also mentioned the provocative behaviour of the suspect during the interrogations, a hectic atmosphere, great emotional pressure on the investigating officers, and the consequences of the crimes for the defendants, particularly the public attention the incident received.

All of this tells us that officials cannot bring themselves to actually authorize torture. No judges are today ready to find arguments to justify torture. This is not just because torture is forbidden under human rights law – something deeper is surely at stake. Quite why the prohibition is so absolute may depend on different ways of seeing the issue. For some, it is simply revolting and unacceptable to treat another human being in a way that is so obviously inhuman; for others, it denies the idea that we have a society and any meaningful sense of law that can protect us from one another. For many, it seems that, even if we accept that in the equation between some temporary pain and preventive life-saving action, the balance may come down in favour of some pain, the wise course is to avoid torture at all times for it risks expanding into general abuse for all sorts of prisoners – generating further resentment and violence aimed at the very population which the torturers seek to protect or save. None of these arguments, however, will convince someone who believes that lives could be saved by using a bit of rough treatment (or torture).

Some commentators feel obliged to weigh in the balance the well-being of the torture victim and the prospect of saving lives. Such an approach does not fit with the current understanding of the absolute ban on torture. Indeed, adherence to the outright ban reveals the extent of our commitment to the underlying values that inform human rights. In the end, I would suggest that it is our twin commitments to democracy and human dignity that underlie the continuing outright prohibition of torture. In the words of the political philosopher Steven Lukes:

> torture is doubly vicious, combining the vice of concealment and
> the vice of violence – specifically violence against the defenceless.
> The first is anti-democratic, preventing us from reaching a
> collective judgment; the second is anti-liberal, constituting, if
> anything does, a violation of dignity of a person.

The rule that prohibits the use of evidence gleaned from torture has been at the centre of concern about detention of suspected terrorists in the recent context of the 'war on terror'. As mentioned above, no one really expects to use evidence extracted through torture to convict those accused of terrorism or kidnapping. The issue that has arisen is whether such information obtained through torture can be used, not for conviction, but for the continuing detention of terrorist suspects in the 'war on terror'. A couple of recent decisions have confirmed the prohibition on the use of any evidence obtained using torture. At the end of 2005, the UK House of Lords delivered a landmark judgment holding that evidence resulting from torture could not be used in proceedings reviewing the legality of the detention of suspected terrorists. A few months later, in 2006, the United States acknowledged, through Military Commissions Instruction No. 10, that it had international human rights obligations under the Torture Convention of 1984, and stated that the Military Commissions may not admit any evidence against an accused established to have been made as a result of torture.

There remain differences of opinion about firstly, whether in cases of doubt as to whether the evidence was obtained using torture, the evidence should be allowed, and, secondly, what should be the burden of proof that should be applied establishing whether particular information was in fact the product of torture. Furthermore, it was conceded in the House of Lords that, even if the judiciary must exclude as evidence information obtained using torture, the executive should be able to rely on this information, as it could be essential to the protection of public safety (see Box 19). Peter King, the Chairman of the US Homeland Security

> **Box 19: Lord Rodger of Earlsferry in *A and others v Home Secretary* (2005)**
>
> Information obtained by torture may be unreliable. But all too often it will be reliable and of value to the torturer and his masters. That is why torturers ply their trade. Sadly, the Gestapo rolled up resistance networks and wiped out their members on the basis of information extracted under torture. Hence operatives sent to occupied countries were given suicide pills to prevent them from succumbing to torture and revealing valuable information about their mission and their contacts. In short, the torturer is abhorred as a *hostis humani generis* not because the information he produces may be unreliable but because of the barbaric means he uses to extract it.

> The premise of this appeal is that, despite the United Nations Convention against Torture and any other obligations under international law, some states still practise torture. More than that, those states may supply information based on statements obtained under torture to the British security services who may find it useful in unearthing terrorist plots. Moreover, when issuing a certificate under section 21 of the 2001 Act, the Secretary of State may have to rely on material that includes such statements.
>
> Mr Starmer QC, who appeared for Amnesty and a number of other interveners, indicated that, in their view, it would be wrong for the Home Secretary to rely on such statements since it would be tantamount to condoning the torture by which the statements were obtained. That stance has the great virtue of coherence; but the coherence is bought at too dear a price. It would mean that the Home Secretary might have to fail in one of the first duties of government, to protect people in this country from potential attack.

Committee, arguing in 2006 against a new legislative ban on cruel, inhuman, and degrading treatment, was reported as saying: 'If we capture Bin Laden tomorrow and we have to hold his head under water to find out where the next attack is going to happen, we ought to be able to do it.' Even if the prohibition of torture remains a cornerstone of human rights, its seems that we still have some way to go before everyone has shaken off the nagging doubt that, some of the time, for some people, the right not to be tortured has to give way to the rights of others to be protected from future violence.

Lastly, let us address the rule that prohibits sending anyone to a country where they run a real risk of being tortured. Here again there is universal agreement on the principle. But in its application we see countervailing forces at work. Asylum-seekers claim they will be tortured on return, immigration authorities question the available evidence, doubt the risk of future torture, and refer to 'diplomatic assurances' from the destination state that torture will not take place. A few well known cases attest to genuine concern from human rights organizations that the practice of believing diplomatic assurances has led to violations of human rights (see Box 20). In 2005, the UN Committee against Torture decided that Sweden had violated

---

Box 20: From the Human Rights Watch 2005 report
Still at Risk: Diplomatic Assurances No Safeguard Against Torture

The U.S. government has also refused to release any information regarding the assurances against torture it claims it received from Syria in the case of Maher Arar. In September 2002, U.S. authorities apprehended Arar, a dual Canadian-Syrian national, in transit from Tunisia through New York to Canada, where he has lived for many years. After holding him for nearly two weeks, and failing to provide him with the ability to effectively challenge his detention or imminent transfer, U.S. immigration authorities flew Arar to Jordan, where he was driven across the border and handed over to Syrian authorities. The transfer was effected despite Arar's repeated statements to U.S. officials that he would be tortured in Syria and his repeated requests to be sent home to Canada. The U.S. government has claimed that prior to Arar's transfer, it obtained assurances from the Syrian government that Arar would not be subjected to torture upon return.

Arar was released without charge from Syrian custody ten months later and has credibly alleged that he was beaten by security officers in Jordan and tortured repeatedly, often with cables and electrical cords, during his confinement in a Syrian prison. The U.S. government has not explained why it

---

sent Arar to Syria rather than to Canada, where he resides, or why it believed Syrian assurances to be credible in light of the government's well-documented record of torture, including designation as a country where torture is a serious abuse by the U.S. Department of State's 2001 (issued March 4, 2002) Country Reports on Human Rights Practices. It remains unclear whether the immigration regulations that should govern cases like Arar's were followed.

11. This cartoon from *The Economist* of 10 June 2006 was published as Swiss Senator Dick Marty of the Council of Europe published his report on 'Alleged secret detentions and unlawful inter-state transfers involving Council of Europe member states'; it evokes the non-cooperation of most European Governments. In September 2006 President Bush acknowledged that the United States had indeed established secret detention centres outside its borders and that the suspects held there had since been transferred to Guantánamo Bay. The European Parliament, in a separate investigation, later complained of the failure of European Governments to cooperate in its investigations of the 'use of European countries by the CIA for the transportation and illegal detention of prisoners'

the international obligation that prohibits sending persons to countries where there is a real risk of torture (see Box 21).

The High Commissioner for Human Rights, Louise Arbour, chose to mark Human Rights Day in 2005 with a statement about torture. She specifically challenged the practice of 'diplomatic assurances':

> There are many reasons to be sceptical about the value of those assurances. If there is no risk of torture in a particular case, they are unnecessary and redundant. If there is a risk, how effective are these assurances likely to be? Assurances that the death penalty will not be sought or imposed are easy to monitor. Not so, I suggest, in the case of torture and ill-treatment. Short of very intrusive and sophisticated monitoring measures, such as around-the-clock video surveillance of the deportee, there is little oversight that could guarantee that the risk of torture will be obliterated in any particular case. While detainees as a group may denounce their torturers if interviewed privately and anonymously, a single individual is unlikely to reveal his ill-treatment if he is to remain under the control of his tormentors after the departure of the 'monitors'.

Box 21: From the UN Committee Against Torture's Decision in *Agiza v Sweden**

13.4 The Committee considers at the outset that it was known, or should have been known, to the State party's authorities at the time of the complainant's removal that Egypt resorted to consistent and widespread use of torture against detainees, and that the risk of such treatment was particularly high in the case of detainees held for political and security reasons. ... The procurement of diplomatic assurances, which, moreover, provided no mechanism for their enforcement, did not suffice to protect against this manifest risk.

Chapter 5
Legitimate restrictions on freedom

The absolute rights discussed so far do not allow for limitations, exceptions, qualifications, or balancing against other rights. Genocide, crimes against humanity, slavery, and torture are simply international crimes, which are prohibited and can be individually punished by any state wherever the acts were committed. The rights we consider in this chapter may, by contrast, be limited through legal restrictions designed to protect a defined legitimate objective. So, for example, liberty can be restricted in the context of the detention of someone following a lawful conviction in a court of law. Freedom of speech is not absolute. As we all know, shouting 'fire' in a crowded theatre can be punished. Although we all should have freedom to receive and impart information, there are obviously legitimate restrictions on passing on commercial or military secrets. Photographs of celebrities may be of interest to a wide readership but their publication may be restricted in order to protect an individual's privacy.

Is it meaningful then to talk about 'rights' in such contexts? You have the right not be detained – until the authorities justify your detention. You have the right to publish – but not if it upsets others. We seem to be merely giving with one hand and taking away with the other. However, the human rights framework applies and is useful. The human rights approach starts from a presumption that we all have rights to liberty, freedom of expression, belief, assembly, association, property, and fair trial. Any restriction on these rights has to be justified as proportionate to the aims pursued by the restriction according to a three-stage schema developed in human rights law (we examine this schema in the next section). The restriction on our freedoms need not be sinister or nefarious. Few contest the need for certain convicted criminals to be deprived of their liberty; introducing human rights in this context enables us to see how we have to start from the presumption that the individual is entitled to liberty unless a fair procedure demonstrates the necessity of incarceration.

Let us start with the right to life and return to freedom from incarceration at the end of this chapter. The right to life would seem at first glance to be absolute, but on closer inspection, it is clear that some deliberate acts which result in the loss of life are not necessarily human rights violations. A police officer, confronted by an armed assailant, may have to shoot in self-defence to save his or her own life or the lives of others. The cases become harder when the danger becomes less imminent. What if a state engages in the targeted assassination of suspected terrorists? Human rights courts have been faced with dozens of complaints that the security forces have used excessive force which was unnecessary in the circumstances. As a general rule, the force used has to be 'proportionate' to the danger to be averted. The UN *Basic Principles on the Use of Force and Firearms by Law Enforcement Officials* states that:

> Law enforcement officials shall not use firearms against persons except in self-defence or defence of others against the imminent threat of death or serious injury, to prevent the perpetration of a particularly serious crime involving grave threat to life, to arrest a person presenting such a danger and resisting their authority, or to prevent his or her escape, and only when less extreme means are insufficient to achieve these objectives. In any event, intentional lethal use of firearms may only be made when strictly unavoidable in order to protect life.

This simple rule is under threat as governments seek to shift the discussion from the context of principles appropriate for a hostage situation, to the realm of anticipatory self-defence to prevent attacks on the nation. It may be helpful here to separate out three proportionality rules which tend to get confused. The first two rules do not authorize limitations on individual freedom – rather they restrict what states may do when they resort to military force.

The first rule concerns how much force can be used by a state in self-defence in response to an armed attack. The answer is that force can be used that is proportionate to repelling the attack if such force is necessary as the only way of averting the attack. This is what is meant by the international law rule that self-defence has to be proportionate and necessary.

The second rule concerns what is increasingly known as 'collateral damage'. It is part of the framework designed to protect the right to life. The law of armed conflict prohibits indiscriminate attacks on civilians. In particular, there is a prohibition on launching an attack which may be expected to cause incidental loss of civilian life which would be excessive in relation to the concrete and direct military advantage anticipated. In other words, the rule demands that the civilian damage has to be proportionate to the military advantage. At a certain point, the collateral damage becomes disproportionate to the military advantage and hence illegal. Those who violate this rule may be tried as war criminals. Examples of prosecutions for violations of this rule are hard to find; we can, however, highlight that the shelling of Sarajevo was successfully prosecuted at the International Criminal Tribunal for the former Yugoslavia. Prosecutor Louise Arbour charged General Galić with a count of attacks against civilians, and he was eventually convicted in 2003 of the war crime of spreading terror among the civilian population as well as crimes against humanity. He was sentenced to 20 years' imprisonment.

The third proportionality rule relates to those human rights that contain built-in limitations on freedom and is dealt with in some detail in the next section. Before looking at these details, it is worth stressing that in thinking about proportionate limitations on human rights, we have to consider what weight we wish to give to the fundamental values that we are seeking to promote through the right in question. The weight we give the right then determines whether or not the restrictions are acceptable. Here we can mention the special role that is often accorded to freedom of speech. The importance that is given to protecting even offensive words is explained by our sense that human progress comes when ideas can be challenged and authority can be questioned. We admit restrictions on speech that incites religious or racial hatred; the problem comes when this principle starts to stifle debate and critical inquiry. The value attached to this freedom can vary in different contexts, with many privileging this right due to its instrumental value for democracy and debate in all spheres of life. The explanation of the special value placed on freedom of expression was captured by the late Najib Mahfous, the Egyptian novelist and Nobel laureate. Writing in 1989 in the context of the threat to kill fellow novelist Salman Rushdie, he stated: 'As regards freedom of expression, I have said that it must be considered sacred and that thought can only be corrected by counter-thought.'

Proportionate limitations on human rights

The concept of *proportionality* is common to determining the limitations on any human rights that can be restricted. These rights can be restricted to the extent that the limit placed on them is proportionate to the aim pursued. A decision maker is obliged to adopt a three-stage process to determine whether the interference with a human right represents a legitimate limitation on the right concerned. This can be summarized as follows:

- is there a legitimate aim to the interference?
- is the interference prescribed by a clear and accessible law?
- is the interference proportionate to the identified legitimate aim and necessary in a democratic society?

So, for example, in a complaint by a Romanian man about secret files kept on him by the government, it was clear that keeping such files for national security purposes was an interference with his right to privacy and, due to the absence of any national law with judicial supervision setting limits to this interference, there had been a violation of the right to respect for private life. If there had been legal safeguards and appropriate judicial supervision of such activity, the interference might have been found to be necessary and proportionate to the aim of protecting national security, and there would have been no violation of human rights (see Box 22).

Box 22: *Rotaru v Romania*

57. The Court notes in this connection that section 8 of Law no. 14/1992 provides that information affecting national security may be gathered, recorded and archived in secret files. No provision of domestic law, however, lays down any limits on the exercise of those powers. Thus, for instance, domestic law does not define the kind of information that may be recorded, the categories of people against whom surveillance measures such as gathering and keeping information may be taken, the circumstances in which such measures may be taken or the procedure to be followed. Similarly, the Law does not lay down limits on the age of information held or the length of time for which it may be kept.

Section 45 empowers the RIS to take over for storage and use the archives that belonged to the former intelligence services operating on Romanian territory and allows inspection of RIS documents with the Director's consent. The Court notes that this section contains no explicit, detailed provision concerning the persons authorised to consult the files, the nature of the files, the procedure to be followed or the use that may be made of the information thus obtained.

58. It also notes that although section 2 of the Law empowers the relevant authorities to permit interferences necessary to prevent and counteract threats to national security, the ground allowing such interferences is not laid down with sufficient precision.

59. The Court must also be satisfied that there exist adequate and effective safeguards against abuse, since a system of secret surveillance designed to protect national security entails the risk of undermining or even destroying democracy on the ground of defending it. ... In order for systems of secret surveillance to be compatible with Article 8 of the Convention, they must contain safeguards established by law which apply to the supervision of the relevant services' activities. Supervision procedures must follow the values of a democratic society as faithfully as possible, in particular the rule of law, which is expressly referred to in the Preamble to the Convention. The rule of law implies, inter alia, that interference by the executive authorities with an individual's rights should be subject to effective supervision, which should normally be carried out by the judiciary, at least in the last resort, since judicial control affords the best guarantees of independence, impartiality and a proper procedure. ...

The human rights approach provides us with more than a slogan. It demands that a government justify its actions in areas that affect the well-being of the individual, and that the justification be in accordance with the rule of law in a democratic society.

Detention

The human rights movement has often concerned itself with those who have been detained for their politics or expressing

THE OBSERVER WEEKEND REVIEW

London, Sunday, May 28, 1961 21

The Forgotten Prisoners

12. *The Observer* announces the Appeal for Amnesty, 28 May 1961. The overwhelming public response led to the eventual founding of Amnesty International

their opinion. Recall the symbolism attributed to the figure of Solzhenitsyn by Kundera in Chapter 1. The founding of Amnesty International in 1961 was prompted by its founder, the barrister Peter Benenson, reading about two Portuguese students publicly raising their glasses in a toast to freedom and then being convicted and sentenced to seven years' imprisonment. *The Observer* newspaper carried Benenson's 'Appeal for Amnesty' under the banner headline 'The Forgotten Prisoners'. This was the culmination of years of reflection and consultation with others on issues related to persecution and imprisonment. The article included photographs of six prisoners: Constantin Noica (a Romanian philosopher), the civil rights supporter the Reverend Ashton from the United States, the Angolan poet Agostinho Neto (held by the Portuguese), Archbishop Beran of Prague, Toni Ambatielos (a trade unionist detained in Greece), and Cardinal Mindszenty of Hungary (taking refuge in the US Embassy in Budapest). Other prisoners from Spain and South Africa were

Human Rights

included in the article. The original Appeal for Amnesty had four aims: to work impartially for the release of those imprisoned for their opinions; to seek for them a fair and public trial; to enlarge the right of asylum and help political refugees to find work; and to urge effective international machinery to guarantee freedom of opinion.

Since that time, Amnesty International has expanded its focus and now explains that its mission is 'to undertake research and action focused on preventing and ending grave abuses of the rights to physical and mental integrity, freedom of conscience and expression, and freedom from discrimination, within the context of its work to promote all human rights'. The original campaigns, however, mobilized public support for a membership-based movement focused on such forgotten prisoners. This is part of the story of the growth of concern for human rights during the Cold War.

Known sometimes as 'prisoners of conscience' or 'political prisoners', such detainees were, and still are, the subjects of human rights campaigns and protests. Their detention has come to be associated with regimes that generally disregard basic freedoms. Such detainees are arrested for expressing political opinions or claiming democratic rights, and their trials are often sorely lacking in the basic elements of a fair trial: the presumption of innocence, access to a lawyer of one's choice, and the chance to challenge the evidence before an independent judge.

A contemporary challenge to detainees' rights concerns the detention of suspected terrorists in the 'global war on terror'. The United States sought in 2006 to explain its detention without trial of terrorist suspects in Guantánamo Bay (Cuba) before the UN Committee against Torture. The United States argued that, although it has detained around 10,000 people since its 2001 war with Afghanistan, it:

only wishes to hold those enemy combatants who are part of or are supporting Taliban or al-Qaida forces (or associated forces) and who, if released, would present a threat of reengaging in belligerent acts or directly aiding and supporting ongoing hostilities against the United States or its allies.

The United States has released about 90% of those it detained in this way, but its report to the UN explains:

> We have made mistakes: of the detainees we have released, we have later recaptured or killed about 5% of them while they were engaged in hostile action against U.S. forces.

The particular situation of the detainees in the US facilities at Guantánamo Bay has been subject to harsh human rights criticism from multiple sources. The UN special procedures recommended that the detainees either be swiftly brought to trial, or released without further delay. As with the discussion concerning torture, there is a continuing risk that the rules which were thought to protect individuals from arbitrary detention are being reinterpreted to allow for considerable flexibility in the context of counter-terrorism. Defenders of the US's policy argue by analogy: because we accept that mentally ill people who pose a danger to society can be incarcerated without having committed any crime, the same logic applies to those labelled as dangerous terrorists. Alternatively, the analogy is made to traditional situations of armed conflict in which combatants and civilians who pose a security threat can be detained without trial. The argument made is that exceptional times call for exceptional measures. The response of human rights advocates is to recall that the idea of human rights was to protect the unpopular and vulnerable from mistreatment and arbitrariness. Suspected terrorists and 'enemy combatants' fit this description. As already stated, the point of human rights thinking is to recognize the worth of an individual human being even when the majority demands a simple sacrifice for the greater good. The technique of human rights is to demand that interferences with individual liberty only be undertaken in accordance with properly constituted legal proceedings.

One of the dangers with focusing on the legitimacy of detention in the Cold War, for political opponents, or for suspected terrorists, is that we lose sight of the bigger picture with regard to those deprived of their liberty. There is a worldwide population of nearly 9 million detainees (see Box 23). The criteria of 'unpopular', 'marginalized', and 'vulnerable' can also be applied to these millions of individuals incarcerated around the world. A huge number of these prisoners are subjected to conditions that fall far short of human rights standards. Writers and diplomats may have lost interest in prisoners in countries such as Russia but the human rights reports of contemporary prison conditions there make grim reading (see Box 24).

> **Box 23: World Prison Population List (6th edn), February 2005***
>
> Over 9 million people are held in penal institutions throughout the world, mostly as pre-trial detainees (remand prisoners) or having been convicted and sentenced. Almost half of these are in the United States (2.09m), China (1.55m plus pre-trial detainees and prisoners in 'administrative detention') or Russia (0.76m).
>
> The United States has the highest prison population rate in the world, some 714 per 100,000 of the national population, followed by Belarus, Bermuda and Russia (all 532), Palau (523), U.S. Virgin Islands (490), Turkmenistan (489), Cuba (487), Suriname (437), Cayman Islands (429), Belize (420), Ukraine (417), Maldive Islands (416), St Kitts and Nevis (415), South Africa (413) and Bahamas (410).

Box 24: US State Department 2005, *Country Report on Human Rights*: Russia*

Prison conditions remained extremely harsh and frequently life-threatening. ... As of July 1, approximately 797,500 persons were in the custody of the criminal justice system, including 48,600 women and 14,500 juveniles.

In 2004 according to official statistics approximately two thousand persons died in SIZOS [pre-trial detention facilities, known as investigation isolation facilities]. Most died as a result of poor sanitary conditions or lack of medical care (the leading cause of death was heart disease). ...

Abuse of prisoners by other prisoners continued to be a problem. Violence among inmates, including beatings and rape, was common. There were elaborate inmate-enforced caste systems in which informers, homosexuals, rapists, prison rape victims, child molesters, and others were considered to be 'untouchable' and were treated very harshly, with little or no protection provided by the prison authorities.

Penal institutions frequently remained overcrowded, but there were reports of some improvements. For example, while many penal facilities remained in urgent need of renovation and upgrading, some reports indicated that these facilities were closer to meeting government standards, which include the provision of four square meters per inmate.

Inmates in the prison system often suffered from inadequate medical care; however, there were some signs of improvement. The Public Council in the MOJ reported that during the 3 years ending in 2004, the number of sick prisoners and detainees decreased by 27 percent. According to the MOJ, as of September 1, 2005, there were approximately 49 thousand tuberculosis-infected persons and 31 thousand HIV-infected persons in SIZOs and correction colonies.

In closing this chapter, we should mention that the right to freedom is in fact now interpreted as a right that continues throughout detention. An individual's freedom is not extinguished on arrest or conviction, the freedom is restricted to the extent that this is necessary. The detaining authority is continually required to re-evaluate the necessity of all detention. Furthermore, the *International Covenant on Civil and Political Rights* demands that prison systems shall have, as an essential aim, reformation and social rehabilitation.

Chapter 6
Balancing rights – the issue of privacy

So far we have resisted the temptation to claim that human rights are about balancing individual freedoms and the collective interests of the community. Such claims say very little about these rights as they melt away into the interests of the majority to live in peace and security. The thrust of international human rights law is that curtailment of rights must be justified by reference to *pre-existing* laws that allow for proportionate action necessary to achieve a legitimate aim (such as national security or public order). We now ought to look at how this formula works in a little more detail, in order to understand when it may indeed be legitimate to 'balance' rights in situations in which rights holders are competing with each other for priority to be given to their interests. We have already seen how, by contrast, the right not to be tortured can be considered to be absolute. We have also seen how the right to freedom under the rule of law may not be spirited away in the face of claims that some individuals appear to be potentially dangerous. Let us now look at some situations in which human rights claims do have to give way in the face of competing interests.

Privacy

Thinking about the notion of privacy forces us to confront fundamental issues at the heart of human rights. Although there is a popular perception that 'time-honoured' rights to privacy are now constantly under attack, it is not at all clear where the notion of privacy came from. If we trace the origin of the concept, we find that privacy is not a traditional constitutional right; one does not find 18th-century revolutionary demands for privacy. In fact, the protection of privacy seems to have developed in an *ad hoc* way in response to feelings of outrage or embarrassment as the need arose. In human rights law, privacy has become a residual right, used to buttress claims that might otherwise be based on respect for dignity, home, correspondence, sexuality, identity, or family. Some might suggest that privacy is a *natural* demand and references are often made to religious texts, which suggest that from ancient times it has been clear that human beings should shield their private parts from public view. But the fact that many people accept that some things, such as nudity, going to the toilet, and sexual activity, should take place in private, rather than in public, does not really help to define where a universal right to privacy comes from, or what it is supposed to protect.

An early reference to a right to privacy can be found in an 1881 case in the United States which arose out of a complaint by a woman that she had been observed against her will during childbirth. Although her complaint succeeded as a case of battery, the court referred to her 'right to the privacy of her apartment'. Further impetus for the right came in the form of a US law review article by Louis Brandeis and Samuel Warren in 1890, called 'The Right to Privacy'. It may be that the inspiration to write the article stemmed from the unwelcome publicity surrounding the wedding of Warren's daughter. In any event, 19th-century preoccupations centred on unauthorized observation or publication. The case studies used by Brandeis and Warren included: an English court's injunction for breach of confidence restraining distribution of etchings made by Prince Albert and Queen Victoria; a French court's protection for the family of an actress, prohibiting the circulation of reproductions of a death-bed portrait; and in

Germany, the seizing of death-bed photos of Bismarck following a request by his children.

As various national laws developed to protect these interests, there was a change in the focus of what needed to be protected by the concept of privacy. By the end of the Second World War, the concerns were different. Early on, Cuba made a proposal for an article protecting privacy in the Universal Declaration of Human Rights. It included three headings: protection of honour, reputation, and correspondence. The focus on the protection of honour and dignity remains in the Inter-American system for the protection of human rights. However, the concerns of the drafters of the Universal Declaration were wider, and the eventual formulation in the Universal Declaration and subsequent treaties covers not only attacks on honour and reputation, but also interference with 'privacy, family, home or correspondence'. In addition, the scope of this protection has been further defined to protect certain aspects of human dignity, which we shall examine in detail below.

Articulating the duties that correspond to this right is hard, as other rights immediately raise their heads in seeming opposition. The right to privacy may extend only to the point where it does not restrict someone else's right to freedom of expression or right to information. The scope of the right to privacy is similarly constrained by the general interest in preventing crime or in promoting public health. However, when we move away from the property-based notion of a right (where the right to privacy would protect, for example, images and personality), to modern notions of private and family life, we find it harder to delimit the right. This is, of course, the strength of the notion of privacy, in that it can adapt to meet changing expectations and technological advances.

In sum, *what* is privacy today? The concept encompasses a claim that we should be unobserved, and that certain information and images about us should not be circulated without our permission. *Why* did these privacy claims arise? They arose because powerful people took offence at such observation. Furthermore, privacy was assimilated to the need to protect the family, home, and correspondence from arbitrary interference and, in addition, there has been a determination to protect honour and reputation. *How* is privacy protected? Historically, privacy was protected by restricting circulation of the damaging material. But if the concept of privacy first became interesting legally as a response to reproductions of images through etchings, photography, and newspapers, more recent technological advances, such as data storage, digital images, DNA identification, retina scans, and the internet, pose new threats to privacy. The right to privacy is now being reinterpreted to meet those challenges.

We might identify at least five contemporary dimensions to privacy. First, there is a desire to be free from observation. We have already mentioned the sense that some of us want to be shielded from others when we are undressed. From this, rights may flow with regard to strip searches, detention, medical situations, hidden cameras, and other forms of surveillance. Second, there is a desire to restrict circulation of information and images about ourselves, especially where knowledge about such information could be embarrassing or prejudicial to our interests. Third, there is an interest in being able to communicate with others without third parties eavesdropping or monitoring our communications. Although the original protection in the human rights treaties covered 'correspondence', the scope of privacy protection has been extended to challenge telephone tapping, monitoring of the sorts of calls made, and most recently, employers' scrutiny of employees' emails. Fourth, our physical and mental well-being needs protection. The law of privacy has been developed to guarantee protection from domestic violence, sexual abuse, corporal punishment, and environmental hazards. Fifth, it is felt that space should be made so that we can develop our personalities free from control. If we are not free to make certain choices about sex, identity, and association then we may fail to develop our personalities to their full potential. In this way, international human rights treaties have been successfully used to challenge laws that criminalized consensual homosexual activity.

Privacy and the attempt to shield the private sphere from human rights protection

But the concept of privacy has another side. Privacy has been used to shield violence against women from interference by law enforcement officials. Privacy has also been invoked as a justification for racial discrimination when hiring domestic staff or excluding people from membership of clubs and associations. The concept of a private sphere free from governmental interference has meant that issues of marital rape, child abuse, and female genital mutilation were not seen as part of the human rights debate, and that dealing with these issues meant invading someone's privacy.

These problems have been compounded by the notion of a public/private divide in law. Many legal systems have evolved around the idea that public law (including human rights protection) should regulate issues concerning governmental authorities, whilst private law regulates disputes between private entities that are not connected to the state or local authorities. By implication, it is sometimes said that private matters are not the business of the public authorities. According to this line of argument, concerns relating to human dignity in this private sphere cannot therefore be remedied through state intervention or recourse to human rights law. Furthermore, to compound this exclusionary policy, international human rights law has been developed through the consideration of *states'* obligations under the various treaties. Because courts and committees can usually only hear complaints against governments, an assumption has arisen that all violations of human rights require the involvement of the government. Violations in the private sphere were simply not considered to be covered by international human rights law.

This has changed. First, the international bodies established under the human rights treaties have interpreted governments' obligations as giving rise to duties to protect individuals even from attacks on their rights by private individuals and other non-state entities. These obligations are often known as positive obligations, or obligations to protect. Second, the development of the law of international crimes has highlighted questions of individual responsibility for violations of international law. The fact is that some of the worst atrocities the international community has to deal with take place without any question of governmental involvement. Obvious examples include the rapes, torture, and civilian massacres carried out by rebel groups. There is now a good argument that such non-state actors have certain human rights obligations. In turn, the scope of human rights obligations is coming to be seen as having an impact on other non-state actors, such as the United Nations and NATO (in the context of their peace operations), international financial institutions (such as the World Bank and the International Monetary Fund), multinational corporations and other forms of businesses, and all sorts of political parties, religious groups, unions, clubs, and associations.

The traditional distinction between public and private, and the consequent exclusion of domestic and family matters from the public sphere, has led to a careful feminist critique of the construction of the public/private divide and its implications for women and women's rights. It has sometimes been suggested that abolishing the notion of a public/private divide is essential to ensure that oppression in the private sphere would be tackled as a matter of public political concern. In particular, it is clear that the human rights discourse traditionally focused on a public sphere and 'forgot' the concerns of women in fields such as armed conflict, development, the workplace, and the family. The solution, however, is not to abolish the right to privacy: privacy claims have proven effective to ensure a degree of control over one's body, one's sexual relations, and over personal information. The way forward is to take women's claims seriously and acknowledge that human rights apply in the private sphere.

Balancing privacy and other values

Balancing the right to privacy with the competing right to freedom of expression is certainly contextual, one might even say cultural. Although the stakes may seem small to some, the example of a newspaper claiming freedom to publish photographs of a famous person with her children helps us to understand the issues. Human rights simultaneously claim to protect freedom of expression and the right to privacy. How to choose? Here we have to admit that the human rights framework is not akin to a set of traffic regulations or simple road rules. There is plenty of room for different people, different judges even, to come to different conclusions, and again everything depends on context. But the disputes are now often argued in terms of weighing different values – and the lexicon of human rights concepts is the vocabulary called upon to articulate the principles at stake.

In a case concerning the publication of photographs of Princess Caroline of Monaco, the judges of the German Federal Constitutional Court were unsympathetic to the claims for breach of privacy – favouring instead the interests protected by press freedom. They saw the need to allow such publication as part of ensuring access to information for all (see Box 25). On the other hand, the judges of the European Court of Human Rights favoured the protection of the Princess's privacy (see Box 26).

The expansion of the concept of privacy to protect one from pollution, including noise pollution, illustrates the point that privacy is not considered an absolute right and that decision makers have a complex task in determining whether an

Box 25: Decision of the Federal Constitutional Court of 15 December 1999, at para 60*

The fact that the press has to fulfil an opinion-forming mission does not exclude entertainment from the constitutional free press guarantee. The formation of opinions does not stand in opposition to entertainment. Entertaining articles can also contribute to the formation of opinions. Such articles can, under certain circumstances, stimulate or influence the formation of opinions in a more sustainable way than information that is exclusively fact-related. Moreover, in the media, an increasing tendency toward the elimination of the distinction between information and entertainment can be observed both with respect to specific organs of the press as a whole as well as with regard to individual articles, i.e., to disseminate information in an entertaining manner or to mix information and entertainment ('infotainment'). This means that many readers obtain the information that they regard as important or interesting exactly from entertaining articles.

interference with the enjoyment of this right is justified. In 2001, residents near Heathrow Airport succeeded in convincing a Chamber of the European Court of Human Rights (by five votes to two) that the noise levels at night were an unjustifiable interference with their effective enjoyment of their right to respect for their homes and their private and family lives. On appeal, the Grand Chamber held by twelve votes to five that the Government had struck the correct balance between the rights of the residents and the rights of others to travel and pursue competitive commercial operations (in turn considered necessary for the 'economic well-being' of the country). The dissenters disagreed and felt the balance had not been properly struck. As they put it:

the close connection between human rights protection and the urgent need for a decontamination of the environment leads us to

> **Box 26: *von Hannover v Germany*, Judgment of the European Court of Human Rights (2004), at paras 76–77***
>
> 76. As the Court has stated above, it considers that the decisive factor in balancing the protection of private life against freedom of expression should lie in the contribution that the published photos and articles make to a debate of general interest. It is clear in the instant case that they made no such contribution since the applicant exercises no official function and the photos and articles related exclusively to details of her private life.
>
> 77. Furthermore, the Court considers that the public does not have a legitimate interest in knowing where the applicant is and how she behaves generally in her private life even if she appears in places that cannot always be described as secluded and despite the fact that she is well known to the public.
>
> Even if such a public interest exists, as does a commercial interest of the magazines in publishing these photos and these articles, in the instant case those interests must, in the Court's view, yield to the applicant's right to the effective protection of her private life.

perceive health as the most basic human need and as pre-eminent. After all, as in this case, what do human rights pertaining to the privacy of the home mean if, day and night, constantly or intermittently, it reverberates with the roar of aircraft engines?

Protecting health as an element of privacy provides one clear dilemma when it is perceived as hindering the convenience of airline travellers and the economy.

With regards to the increasing use of closed-circuit surveillance cameras, DNA and other genetic information, the same questions we discussed earlier must be asked. Is there a legitimate aim?

13. The European Court of Human Rights ruled that Princess Caroline of Monaco's rights had been violated in the context of the publication of photographs taken by paparazzi. The German courts had given priority to freedom of expression and information

Are the interferences authorized by an accessible law, and are they really necessary in a democratic society to protect the community from crime and threats to national security? There are fears that such data will be used by employers and insurance companies to detect those likely to have future health problems, thus introducing an unacceptable level of discrimination based on predicted future misfortune.

The priority given to privacy depends on the context and, to some extent, the weight that a particular society or decision-making body wishes to accord such a claim. It is perhaps helpful to recall a primary purpose of protecting privacy, which is to allow for the development of the personality in relation to others without unnecessary interference. Where the protection of privacy is being invoked to shield public officials from criticism, to seal off violence in the domestic arena from official protection, or to justify racial or other types of prohibited discrimination, then we should be alert to the appropriation of the concept of privacy to assist in the denial of human rights. The right to privacy has forged important advances in the international protection of human rights – but it simultaneously remains a tool that can easily be invoked to undermine other rights. Claims that privacy is under threat are set to continue for some time; how much weight they are accorded will depend on what is considered to be at stake.

Chapter 7
Food, education, health, housing, and work

'Human rights begin with breakfast': this quip from the former President of Senegal, Léopold Senghor, prompts many to react in alarm. Some see this assertion as part of an argument that certain rights, such as the right to food, need to be properly secured before one can turn to the luxury of the right to vote or to the privilege of freedom of expression. Indeed, many subscribe to a so-called 'full belly thesis', according to which subsistence rights to food and water have to be secured before turning to civil and political rights relating to political participation, arbitrary detention, freedom of expression, or privacy. Such argumentation is not as prevalent as it used to be (at least in government circles). Today all governments accept (most of the time) that there should be no prioritization among different types of rights. Different types of rights are seen to be mutually reinforcing: better nutrition, health and education will lead to improvements in political freedoms and the rule of law; similarly, freedom of expression and association can ensure that the best decisions are taken to protect rights to food, health, and work. Despite the logic of such a desire to secure 'all rights for all people', traditional assumptions about what constitute 'proper' human rights still persist. One does not have to look very far to find voices claiming that the rights we are discussing in this next chapter are not really human rights (see Box 27). Such an approach probably conceals a sense that such rights get in the way of rational choice

> **Box 27: *The Economist,* 18 August 2001, 'Righting Wrongs'**
>
> **Designating a good as a universal human right means that reasonable people believe that under no jurisdiction, and under no circumstances, may that good be justly denied to anybody. Although freedom from torture certainly now falls into this category – arguably due to the efforts of groups like Amnesty – goods such as food and a decent home do not. Governments may intentionally torture their citizens; they do not usually intentionally inflict on them poverty and ill-health. The moral imperative to stop poverty or disease is therefore not as convincing as the moral imperative to stop torture.**

and economic efficiency. Alternatively, those who wish to confine human rights to issues such as torture and freedom of expression may have simply underestimated how much we now care about poverty and disease, not only when it affects us – but also when it affects other people.

The traditional narrow reading of human rights is, today, rarely explicitly defended in international relations. The expression 'human rights' covers not only civil and political rights such as freedom from torture, slavery, and arbitrary detention, but also economic, social, and cultural rights. In the words of the Universal Declaration:

> Everyone has the right to a standard of living adequate for the
> health and well-being of himself and of his family, including food,
> clothing, housing and medical care and necessary social services,
> and the right to security in the event of unemployment, sickness,
> disability, widowhood, old age or other lack of livelihood in
> circumstances beyond his control.

International disagreement now concerns, first, the appropriate mechanisms for the enforcement of such rights, and second, the exact scope of these rights. Before turning to the interpretation of the scope of these rights, let us consider the perceived problem of enforcement.

A main concern is that economic and social policy is best determined by policy makers who are democratically accountable, and not by unelected judges with no specialized knowledge of how to prioritize the distribution of limited resources. In a context such as health, it is clear that health authorities and hospitals may have to deny some people treatment when this represents an unreasonable strain on limited resources. Those who support increasing the judicial enforcement of economic, social, and cultural rights point out that protecting civil and political rights also involves deciding questions with resource implications: the provision of humane conditions for detainees has resource implications; establishing the pre-conditions for truly free and fair elections likewise costs money. But there remains a tension regarding the appropriateness of economic and social rights for judicial enforcement. The result is that, in those instances when courts have adjudicated economic, social, and cultural rights, judges have been careful not to impinge overly on the roles of the legislature and executive. For example, the judiciary in South Africa has reminded the Government of its duty to justify restrictions on access to health care, and demanded that the Government develops policies to ensure housing for the most marginalized. As with civil and political rights, the judiciary may remind governments that they have duties to ensure that legislation is introduced to ensure that rights can be enjoyed and protected under an effective legal system. Let us now look at some economic and social rights in a little more detail.

Food

The existence of the right to food does not mean that the government has to provide free food for all. The right to food is shorthand for a more complex set of obligations relating to 'food security' which involves ensuring access to food and planning for shortages and distribution problems. We can start with the immediate obligations. First, the government should avoid undermining food security and should plan for the needs of the population. In particular, there should be no violation of the right to food through the unjustified destruction of crops or evictions from land. Furthermore, there must be no discrimination with regard to access to food. These immediate obligations can be seen as part of a duty to *respect* the right to food.

A second level of obligation concerns the duty to *protect* the right to food. Here we find obligations to protect individuals from interference with their right to food from other actors. So, for example, the state may have a duty to regulate with regard to food safety. In some contexts, this may require the state to guarantee that title to land is ensured to those who have a close cultural link to the land – such as indigenous peoples.

The third level is variously expressed as an obligation to fulfil, assist, facilitate, or provide. This means, on the one hand, strengthening access to food by ensuring that people have the resources for food security through stimulating employment, engaging in land reform, and developing transport and storage facilities. On the other hand, the state may have to provide food or social security to fulfil basic needs in the situations referred to in the Universal Declaration (cited above) in which the individual is subject to 'unemployment, sickness, disability, widowhood, old age or other lack of livelihood in circumstances beyond his control'.

These international obligations have been developed in tandem with constitutional rights in some countries. Significant progress has been made through national civil society appeals to the right to food in public interest litigation before the Indian Supreme Court. Kamayani Bali Mahabal from the Centre for Enquiry into

Health and Allied Themes (CEHAT, the acronym, is Hindi for health) explains:

> The Right to Food Campaign (the Campaign) operates on the premise that everyone has a fundamental right to be free from hunger and under-nutrition. Realising this right requires not only equitable and sustainable food systems, but also a guarantee of livelihood security such as the right to work, land and social security. The Campaign pursues its goals through a wide range of activities, including initiating public hearings, action-orientated research, media advocacy and lobbying, as well as participating in public interest litigation on the right to food. In relation to the latter activity, the Campaign has a small 'legal support group' which handles Supreme Court hearings ... Also, the 'mid-day meal movement' has continued to grow. According to official data, 50 million children now get a free school lunch, with another 50 million or so in the queue.

In recent years, considerable focus has been placed on the 'right to water' as water has come to be regarded as a part of a globalized services market. Often subsumed under the right to food, the right to water is increasingly raised in the context of privatization of public utilities, and in particular with regard to multinational companies which have been accused of pricing parts of the population out of the market, resulting in a denial of the right to water (see Box 28).

Education

'Education makes a people easy to lead, but difficult to drive; easy to govern, but impossible to enslave.' This comment, attributed to the Member of Parliament and Lord Chancellor Baron Brougham (1778–1868), reminds us that education is essential to any effort to enhance human rights. In this sense, the right to education is crucial to empowering people to be able to enjoy their other rights. The right to education involves not only obligations to

> ### Box 28: J. Shultz, 'Bringing It All Back Home'
>
> No example illustrates the enduring power of a good story better than Cochabamba, Bolivia's public revolt against privatisation of its water system. Here the evils of economic globalization, and the valiant fight against them, were played out in living color. The World Bank used all the powers at its disposal to pressure the Bolivian Government to lease off its water system to a transnational corporation and it did so, to a subsidiary of the powerful US-based, Bechtel Corporation. Within weeks Bechtel had doubled and tripled people's water rates, sending a mass movement of urban and rural water users into the streets. This culminated in a weeklong general strike, the forced departure of the corporation and the return of the water system to public hands. In December 2001 Bechtal announced it was suing the Bolivian government for $25 million for breaking the water contract.
>
> During the water wars, Tanya Paredes, a mother who supports her four children by knitting baby clothes, became an international symbol after it was reported that her 300-per-cent water bill increase totalled more than what it cost to feed her family for a week. Even people who have never heard of the World Bank and don't have feelings one way or another towards Bechtel could grasp in an instant that something about globalization had gone horribly wrong.

refrain from interfering with the right by closing schools, or discriminating against certain pupils, but also includes obligations to fulfil the right to education by providing compulsory, free primary education for all. The right to education has been developed at the doctrinal level to encompass what is known as a '4As' approach: availability, accessibility, acceptability, and adaptability. (Some might hear echoes here of the 3Rs – reading, writing, and arithmetic.)

First, education has to be *available* in a functional sense so that, in the words of the UN Committee on Economic Social and Cultural Rights, there has to be: 'protection from the elements, sanitation facilities for both sexes, safe drinking water, trained teachers receiving domestically competitive salaries, [and] teaching materials.' The late UN expert Katerina Tomaševski pointed out that for availability to be meaningful, rather than formal, schools have actually to attract children. Not only must schools be formally open to both boys and girls, but they should be monitored to ensure that girls and boys are retained in school. Inadequate teaching or lack of relevant schoolbooks will mean that children and parents will see little point in using the available facilities, and the government will fail in its obligation to provide compulsory primary education that is available free to all.

Second, the state must ensure that schools and programmes are *accessible* to all. This has three dimensions. First, accessibility means *non-discrimination*. This is an obligation on states with immediate effect. Affirmative action, or 'temporary special measures', intended to bring about equality for men and women, or for disadvantaged groups, is not considered a violation of the non-discrimination rule as long as it does not continue unnecessarily. Discrimination against girls remains a real problem. For example, pregnancy can trigger girls being expelled from school in violation of their right to education. Furthermore, for some parents, it is seen as economically irrational to invest in their daughters' education; they therefore privilege their boys' education. The second dimension to accessibility is *physical accessibility*. This means that children with disabilities are not excluded due to the design of the buildings, and that education is within physical reach geographically. The third dimension is *economic accessibility*. While international law demands that education be free in the elementary and fundamental stages, there is a weaker obligation with regard to secondary education so that there should be a progression towards free secondary education. This means that, although priority is to be given to ensuring free primary education, governments must also take concrete steps to ensure free secondary and tertiary education.

Acceptability is the concept used to describe the importance of ensuring that education is conducted in a way that is acceptable to children and parents. The environment has to tackle not only material conditions, and aspects such as violence and scheduling, but it must also enable children to develop and learn. Corporal punishment in schools is a violation of the rights of the child, and bullying can be addressed in terms of human rights language which refers to cruel, inhuman, and degrading treatment.

From the earliest international articulation of the right to education, there has been a second dimension relating to parents' rights in education: the rights of parents to choose the kind of education to be given to their children. Parents have also used this human right to challenge national laws on corporal punishment in schools. Where Christian schools in South Africa claimed that banning corporal punishment in schools violated the human rights of parents to practise their religion under the Constitution, the Constitutional Court considered how to weigh respect for this right with the interests of the child. The Court brought the balance down firmly in favour of upholding the general ban on corporal punishment; the law banning corporal punishment was held to be designed to promote respect for the dignity and physical integrity of all children (see Box 29). The use of corporal punishment in Scotland was also successfully challenged before the European Court of Human Rights, where it held that the parents' philosophical convictions regarding discipline of their children are only protected when they are worthy of respect in a democratic society and are compatible with human dignity and the right to education of the child.

The fourth aspect of the right to education, the concept of *adaptability*, raises fundamental questions about education. What is education for? And who decides? As long as education is geared

> **Box 29: *Christian Education South Africa v Minister of Education****
>
> The overlap and tension between the different clusters of rights reflect themselves in contradictory assessments of how the central constitutional value of dignity is implicated. On the one hand, the dignity of the parents may be negatively affected when the state tells them how to bring up and discipline their children and limits the manner in which they may express their religious beliefs. The child who has grown up in the particular faith may regard the punishment, although hurtful, as designed to strengthen his character. On the other hand, the child is being subjected to what an outsider might regard as the indignity of suffering a painful and humiliating hiding deliberately inflicted on him in an institutional setting. Indeed, it would be unusual if the child did not have ambivalent emotions. It is in this complex factual and psychological setting that the matter must be decided.

solely to admission to the next (selective) stage of education, some children will be ill-equipped for life. Article 29 of the Convention on the Rights of the Child sets out a number of aims for education. The stress is on developing the child's personality and instilling respect for particular values, including the protection of the environment (see Box 30).

Health

The right to health does not mean that we have the right to be healthy. The right to health is defined by UN expert Paul Hunt as:

> a right to an effective and integrated health system, encompassing health care and the underlying determinants of health, which is responsive to national and local priorities, and accessible to all.

Box 30: Convention on the Rights of the Child*

Art. 29 (1) States Parties agree that the education of the child shall be directed to:

(a) The development of the child's personality, talents and mental and physical abilities to their fullest potential;

(b) The development of respect for human rights and fundamental freedoms, and for the principles enshrined in the Charter of the United Nations;

(c) The development of respect for the child's parents, his or her own cultural identity, language and values, for the national values of the country in which the child is living, the country from which he or she may originate, and for civilizations different from his or her own;

(d) The preparation of the child for responsible life in a free society, in the spirit of understanding, peace, tolerance, equality of sexes, and friendship among all peoples, ethnic, national and religious groups and persons of indigenous origin;

(e) The development of respect for the natural environment.

He uses the *accessibility* prism to point out that the right to health means that health care:

> must be accessible to all, not just the wealthy, but also those living in poverty; not just majority ethnic groups, but minorities and indigenous peoples, too; not just those living in urban areas, but also remote villagers; not just men, but also women. The health system has to be accessible to all disadvantaged individuals and communities.

The UN Committee on Economic, Social and Cultural Rights has developed an interpretation of the right to health contained in the UN Covenant. They use the same triptych of obligations to respect, protect, and fulfil that we discussed earlier. Their interpretation can be summarized as follows.

First, the obligation to *respect* requires states to avoid measures that could prevent the enjoyment of the right. Therefore, states are under the obligation to *respect* the right to health by, *inter alia*, refraining from (i) denying or limiting equal access for all persons to preventive, curative, and palliative health services; (ii) prohibiting or impeding traditional preventive care, healing practices, and medicines; (iii) marketing unsafe drugs; (iv) applying coercive medical treatments; (v) limiting access to contraceptives and other means of maintaining sexual and reproductive health; and (vi) censoring, withholding, or intentionally misrepresenting health-related information, including sexual education and information, as well as preventing people's participation in health-related matters.

Second, the obligation to *protect* requires states to take measures that prevent third parties from interfering with the right to adequate health care. Obligations to *protect* include, therefore, the duties of states to (1) adopt legislation or to take other measures ensuring equal access to health care and health-related services provided by third parties; (ii) ensure that privatization of the health sector does not constitute a threat to the availability, accessibility, acceptability and quality of health facilities, goods and services; (iii) control the marketing of medical equipment and medicines by third parties; (iv) prevent third parties from coercing women to undergo traditional practices, such as female genital mutilation; and (v) take measures to protect all vulnerable or marginalized groups of society, in particular women, children, adolescents, and older persons.

Finally, the obligation to *fulfil* requires states to take positive measures that enable individuals and groups to enjoy the right to health. The obligation to *fulfil* requires states, for instance, to

(i) give sufficient recognition to the right to health in the national, political, and legal systems, preferably by way of legislative implementation; (ii) adopt a national health policy with a detailed plan for realizing the right to health; (iii) ensure provision of health care, including immunization programmes against the major infectious diseases; (iv) ensure equal access for all to the underlying determinants of health, such as nutritiously safe food and potable drinking water, basic sanitation, and adequate housing and living conditions; (v) ensure the appropriate training of doctors and other medical personnel, the provision of sufficient numbers of hospitals, clinics, and other health-related facilities with due regard to equitable distribution throughout the country; (vi) provide a public, private, or mixed health insurance system that is affordable for all; (vii) promote medical research and health education; and (viii) promote information campaigns, in particular with respect to HIV/AIDS, sexual and reproductive health, traditional practices, domestic violence, the abuse of alcohol, and the use of cigarettes, drugs, and other harmful substances.

This all looks perfect on paper, and left to their own devices, most governments would claim they are doing their best to progressively realize all of the above, taking into account their available resources. Hunt and others have therefore started to develop an accountability schema using indicators and benchmarks. This is how it works. First, key indicators are chosen. These should be disaggregated for gender or race, or other relevant characteristics as appropriate. The challenge is to ensure that all agencies and human rights bodies concentrate on equivalent indicators. The second step is for the government to set national benchmarks as a time-bound target. The government would propose various national benchmarks. The relevant treaty monitoring body should approve or adjust the benchmark to ensure that the state fulfils its international obligations in this context. Lastly, as part of any periodic review, these benchmarks are reviewed by the various international and national actors concerned and, in this way, progress or regression can be monitored and, if necessary, corrected. (See Box 31 for more detail.)

Here we are not really in the presence of judicially enforceable remedies for violations of rights; we are in the realm of thinking about issues such as health or trade or development in terms of a rights-based approach which focuses on concepts such as participation, accountability, non-discrimination, empowerment, and links to international legal norms.

A contemporary controversy in the context of the right to health is the perceived clash with the intellectual property rights of multinational pharmaceutical companies. While states may have a duty under some legal regimes to protect intellectual property rights in ways that ensure the welfare of the society, intellectual property rights are not absolute human rights like the right not to be tortured. The interests of companies in earning enough from sales of their pharmaceuticals to enable them to fund further research and development have to be weighed by the state against the human rights of those needing access to health care. So far, this issue has remained a question of political action rather than a judicial weighing of competing rights. A successful popular campaign was mounted against those pharmaceutical companies that sought to sue the South African Government of Nelson Mandela for the Government's failure to protect their intellectual property rights. In a related development, states have agreed, in the context of the international trade regime of the World Trade Organization (WTO), on trade law rules (designed to protect intellectual property rights) accommodating the obligation on states to provide accessible health care. Under a new procedure, generic medicines manufactured under compulsory licences can be imported and used by states in need. Access to essential medicines remains, however, a huge challenge. At the end of 2005, only 17% of those in need of anti-retroviral HIV treatment in Sub-Saharan Africa had access to these medicines. The G8

Box 31: 2006 Report of the Special Rapporteur on the Right of Everyone to the Enjoyment of the Highest Attainable Standard of Physical and Mental Health, Paul Hunt, paras 40–2*

Sexual and reproductive health are integral elements of the right to health. So States need a way of measuring whether or not they are progressively realizing sexual and reproductive health. There are many relevant indicators, including the proportion of births attended by skilled health personnel. A State may select this indicator as one of those it uses to measure its progressive realization of sexual and reproductive health rights.

The national data may show that the proportion of births attended by skilled health personnel is 60 per cent. When disaggregated on the basis of rural/urban, data may reveal that the proportion is 70 per cent in urban centres, but only 50 per cent in rural areas. When further disaggregated on the basis of ethnicity, data may also show that coverage in the rural areas is uneven: the dominant ethnic group enjoys a coverage of 70 per cent but the minority ethnic group only 40 per cent. This highlights the crucial importance of disaggregation as a means of identifying de facto discrimination. When disaggregated, the indicator confirms that women members of the ethnic minority in rural areas are especially disadvantaged and require particular attention.

Consistent with the progressive realization of the right to health, the State may decide to aim for a uniform national coverage of 70 per cent, in both the urban and rural areas and for all ethnic groups, in five years' time. Thus, the indicator is the proportion of births attended by skilled health personnel and the benchmark or target is 70 per cent. The State will formulate and implement policies and programmes that are designed to reach the benchmark of 70 per cent in five years.

> The data show that the policies and programmes will have
> to be specially designed to reach the minority ethnic group
> living in the rural areas.

leaders pledged in Scotland in 2005 that there should be as near
as possible universal access to HIV treatment by 2010. Later
in the year, all states agreed at the UN Summit that everyone,
including the pharmaceutical companies, should work to ensure
such access and to provide the necessary drugs to rid the African
continent of tuberculosis and malaria (see Box 32).

Housing

We have just seen that the right to health does not mean that an
individual can demand unlimited resources from the government.
Similarly, Scott Leckie, in one of his core contributions to the
topic, starts out by assuring the reader that 'The legal texts
establishing housing rights norms obviously were not created

> **Box 32: UN General Assembly 2005 Summit
> Outcome, para 68(i)***
>
> To provide, with the aim of an AIDS-, malaria- and
> tuberculosis-free generation in Africa, assistance for
> prevention and care and to come as close as possible to
> achieving the goal of universal access by 2010 to HIV/AIDS
> treatment in African countries, to encourage pharmaceutical
> companies to make drugs, including antiretroviral drugs,
> affordable and accessible in Africa and to ensure increased
> bilateral and multilateral assistance, where possible on
> a grant basis, to combat malaria, tuberculosis and other
> infectious diseases in Africa through the strengthening of
> health systems.

to ensure the right of everyone to inhabit a luxurious mansion, surrounded by well sculpted gardens.' It is the concept of *adequacy* that has been central to the development of the right to housing since its inclusion in the Universal Declaration of Human Rights in 1948. This concept takes us beyond a minimal notion of shelter, the roof over one's head, and focuses our attention on the crucial concerns of the individual holders of the right (see Box 33).

Worldwide the housing situation is dire, with the UN estimating that 600 million urban dwellers and over one billion rural dwellers live in overcrowded and poor-quality housing with inadequate provision of water, sanitation, drainage, and garbage collection.

Box 33: The 1996 UN Conference on Human Settlements (Habitat Agenda) para. 60

Adequate shelter means more than a roof over one's head. It also means adequate privacy; adequate space; physical accessibility; adequate security; security of tenure; structural stability and durability; adequate lighting, heating and ventilation; adequate basic infrastructure, such as water-supply, sanitation and waste-management facilities; suitable environmental quality and health-related factors; and adequate and accessible location with regard to work and basic facilities: all of which should be available at an affordable cost. Adequacy should be determined together with the people concerned, bearing in mind the prospect for gradual development. Adequacy often varies from country to country, since it depends on specific cultural, social, environmental and economic factors. Gender-specific and age-specific factors, such as the exposure of children and women to toxic substances, should be considered in this context.

The UN Committee on Economic, Social and Cultural Rights has paid particular attention to the right to adequate housing (as found in the Covenant on Economic, Social and Cultural Rights) and addressed the question of *adequacy* in some detail, highlighting the following aspects: (i) legal security of tenure; (ii) availability of services, materials, facilities, and infrastructure; (iii) affordability; (iv) habitability; (v) accessibility; (vi) location; (vii) cultural adequacy. With regard to the immediate obligation of governments, there is clearly an obligation to abstain from practices that are discriminatory, or that involve illegal forced evictions.

Let us look at legal security of tenure. Tenure is a flexible institution, which can take different forms in different contexts. The Committee includes: 'rental (public and private) accommodation, cooperative housing, lease, owner-occupation, emergency housing and informal settlements, including occupation of land or property'. There has also been an interest in security of tenure from economists and those working in development. This right is not only about the protection of dignity, but can in addition be seen as instrumental to economic development. We should also consider, however, that property rules may be part of the problem rather than a simple solution. For example, in many countries property is registered in the man's name alone, often limiting women's access to housing in the event of death or divorce.

Perhaps the greatest focus in this area has been on the legal and procedural protections that have to be developed in the context of 'forced evictions' as defined in human rights law. The general prohibition on forced evictions is an obligation of immediate obligation. The Committee has defined forced evictions as follows:

> the permanent or temporary removal against their will of individuals, families and/or communities from the homes and/or land which they occupy, without the provision of, and access to,

appropriate forms of legal or other protection. The prohibition
on forced evictions does not, however, apply to evictions carried
out by force in accordance with the law and in conformity with
the provisions of the International Covenants on Human Rights.

This immediate obligation is now at the heart of housing rights
activism. Part of the focus has been on large-scale development
projects. In turn, this has prompted the adoption of guidelines
on involuntary resettlement by the Organization for Economic
Cooperation and Development, as well as by the World Bank.

These elaborate guidelines, norms, and recommendations have,
in some cases, been used to prevent or halt forced evictions
and remind governments that housing is a human rights issue.
But things are not really so simple. As with other rights, such
as the right to privacy, housing rights come up against other
fundamental rights claims. Consider the right to water of the
people of Gujarat and the rights of those about to be displaced
from their housing in the area designated to be flooded for
the Narmada dam in India. Invoking human rights does not
determine the dilemma. Human rights principles, however,
provide the vocabulary for the evaluation of the decision-making
process. The majority of the Indian Supreme Court was careful
to avoid replacing the government's decisions with a judicial
preference for one set of rights claims.

> Conflicting rights had to be considered. If for one set of people
> namely those of Gujarat, there was only one solution, namely,
> construction of a dam, the same would have an adverse effect on
> another set of people whose houses and agricultural land would be
> submerged in water ... When a decision is taken by the Government
> after due consideration and full application of mind, the Court is
> not to sit in appeal over such decision.

In closing this section on housing, we should point out that some
actions against the right to housing amount to international

crimes and now give rise to individual criminal responsibility. Starting with the crimes mentioned in the Rome Statute for the International Criminal Court, we could mention that a widespread or systematic attack against the civilian population involving the deportation or forced transfer of persons constitutes an international crime against humanity. Of direct relevance are war crimes involving the destruction of housing. The law here is complex and recognizes that there will be some necessary damage in times of armed conflict, but one might mention three separate international war crimes.

- First, the war crime of extensive destruction and appropriation of property by an Occupying Power, not justified by military necessity, and carried out unlawfully and wantonly;
- Second, in an international armed conflict, the war crime of intentionally launching an attack in the knowledge that such attack will cause incidental loss of life or injury to civilians or damage to civilian objects which would be clearly excessive in relation to the concrete and direct overall military advantage anticipated;
- Third, in the context of civil wars, destroying or seizing the property of an adversary unless such destruction or seizure is imperatively demanded by the necessities of the conflict.

Those who order, facilitate, or carry out such destruction of housing commit war crimes and could be prosecuted, not just in a relevant international criminal tribunal, but in the courts of any state willing to bring such suspected war criminals to justice.

Work

Various national and local struggles for workers' rights have encompassed the fight against slavery and forced labour, claims for decent working conditions and fair wages, the right to form and join trade unions, and the right to strike. In some ways, these movements antedate the human rights movement. International standards and procedures were elaborated through the work of the International Labour Organization (ILO), established in 1919 at the end of the First World War, and against the background of the Russian Revolution. At that time, an international focus was regarded as crucial to counterbalance the increasing appeal of an advancing Communism promising to vindicate workers' rights. Social justice was seen in the context of both World Wars as essential to achieve lasting peace. The ILO developed detailed Conventions and elaborate mechanisms for monitoring compliance with the various standards.

A new era began in 1998, with a divisive discussion about protecting workers' rights through the WTO international trade law regime. As already mentioned in the chapter on foreign policy, there was considerable unease that introducing labour rights issues through a social clause into the trade regime would allow richer states to exclude imports from developing countries on the grounds that workers in those countries were neither properly paid nor afforded the sorts of labour rights they would enjoy in the West. Developing countries would thereby be precluded from enjoying the economic benefits of their comparative advantage in cheap labour. It was decided that the issue of workers' rights should be shunted out of the trade arena and left to the ILO. The ILO responded by taking a fresh look at international labour rights. The rights were then streamlined and repackaged in the ILO Declaration on Fundamental Principles and Rights at Work. The principles are said to be:

- freedom of association and the effective recognition of the right to collective bargaining;
- the elimination of all forms of forced or compulsory labour;
- the effective abolition of child labour; and
- the elimination of discrimination in respect of employment and occupation.

14. Senator Edward Kennedy addressing a workers' rights rally on Human Rights Day, 10 December 2003

This reductive approach: first from over a hundred Conventions down to a few standards; then from rights to 'principles', has been met with suspicion in some quarters. Defenders of the new approach reply that the other rights have in no way been diminished, highlighting core labour standards simply renders those rights more visible and effective.

What exactly is the right to work? The UN Committee on Economic, Social and Cultural Rights has warned: 'The right to work should not be understood as an absolute and unconditional right to obtain employment.' Like some of the other rights we have been considering in this chapter, the idea evoked by the right does not in fact give rise to an obvious immediate entitlement. The package of component rights is complicated. The first right is the right not to be subjected to forced labour. A second right demands that there should be access to the employment market. Third, there should be safe working conditions and just remuneration. Fourth, the right to form trade unions must be recognized; and fifth, workers have the right not to be discriminated against, and to be protected from unfair dismissal. Finally, everyone has the right to social security in the event of unemployment.

Of course, some of the limitations we encountered in previous chapters will apply. Trade union rights may arguably be limited where this is necessary to protect national security: and this reasoning was successfully relied upon by the British Government in the 1980s to uphold its ban on trade unions at its intelligence 'listening post' known as GCHQ. Similarly, states may be able to introduce certain restrictions on access to the labour market by foreigners (migrant workers); although once granted employment, there can usually be no excuse for discrimination against foreigners.

Human rights have not always been regarded as supportive of the aspirations of the trade union movement. Judges have considered the right to form trade unions to include a 'negative right of association' entitling workers to refuse to join a trade union. There have been attempts to present strike action or boycotts by trade union members as violations by the striking workers of a right of employers to refuse to enter into agreements with trade unions.

While the principles of freedom of association at work and protection from unfair dismissal may be universally recognized, the detail of how these rights are implemented is dependent on ideology, political power, and cultural context. Some countries have a long tradition of recognizing the importance of giving trade unions a central role in negotiating working conditions; others see unions as a hindrance to flexibility and competitiveness. Such approaches are not fixed and can change in response to social changes and the emergence of new majorities through the democratic process. The principle of freedom of association remains intact. The challenge comes in particular from arguments that globalization has rendered those entities (states and businesses) that respect labour rights uncompetitive. There is a fear that commitment to labour rights can act as a disincentive to foreign investment. In some countries the response has been to create special 'export processing zones' (see Box 34). In fact, the Organization for Economic Cooperation and Development has concluded, based on studies published in 1996 and 2000, that 'countries with low core labour standards do not enjoy better export performance than high-standard countries'. We might point out here that consumers and ethical investors are becoming increasingly sensitive to the working conditions of those in the supply chain for certain goods in the garment and footwear sectors. This interest in working conditions can also be found with regard to workers' rights in the coffee, tea, cocoa, sugar, and mining sectors.

Regional integration, in contexts such as the European Union, has driven a degree of harmonization of labour rights in order to ensure fair competition in the internal market. The economic logic of ensuring a level playing field in Europe has led, not only

Box 34: Naomi Klein, *No Logo*

The Philippine government... says that the zones are subject to the same labor standards as the rest of Philippine society: workers must be paid the minimum wage, receive social security benefits, have some measure of job security, be dismissed only with just cause and be paid extra for overtime, and they have the right to form independent trade unions. But in reality, the government views working conditions in the export factories as a matter of foreign trade policy, not a labor-rights issue. And since the government attracted foreign investors with promises of a cheap and docile workforce, it intends to deliver. For this reason, labor department officials turn a blind eye to violations in the zone or even facilitate them.

to concrete rules ensuring equal pay for men and women at work, but also to protection concerning harassment in the workplace. Furthermore, EU law has developed to demand prohibitions on racial and religious discrimination, as well as on discrimination in the workplace on the grounds of disability, age, and sexual orientation. We now turn to deal with discrimination in a little more detail.

Chapter 8
Discrimination and equality

As we have seen throughout this short book, discrimination is prohibited with regard to the enjoyment of all rights. We have discovered the immediate obligation to prevent discrimination, not only in the context of the enjoyment of civil and political rights (such as personal freedom from arbitrary detention, freedom of expression, political participation, and association), but also in the fields of food, health, education, housing, and work. Now we shall consider the prohibited grounds of discrimination, what new grounds may be emerging, and when drawing distinctions between people can be considered reasonable and therefore legitimate.

For some, the foundation of human rights can be traced to the twin ideas that human beings are born equal in dignity and rights, and that all human beings have to be treated with equal concern and respect. Quite why we should treat others in this way and exactly how far we should go to ensure that they are shown this respect remain tricky questions for moral philosophers. These discussions usually come close to admitting that there is something 'sacred' about each individual human being, and that despite the existence of obvious inequalities at birth, justice and fairness demand that we design a system to give everyone equal access to opportunities and, in some versions, redistribute resources to ensure that the least well-off are prioritized in our attempts to achieve equality of outcomes. These philosophical approaches to human rights provide much of the ballast for the human rights rules on discrimination, and provide the moral case for developing these rules to achieve greater social justice on a global scale.

Another way to look at non-discrimination is through the lens of the campaigns and activists who built the human rights movement: anti-slavery, the fight for women's rights, anti-colonialism, anti-apartheid, anti-racism. Discrimination is also central to the concept of genocide. The injustice that stems from being treated adversely on account of one's gender, colour, or religion formed the human right to non-discrimination in its present form. The Universal Declaration of Human Rights proclaimed in 1948 that:

> Everyone is entitled to all the rights and freedoms set forth in this Declaration, without distinction of any kind, such as race, colour, sex, language, religion, political or other opinion, national or social origin, property, birth or other status.

The first thing to notice is that the ban on discrimination was limited to the enjoyment of the other rights in the Declaration. Since that time, international and national rules have extended the scope of non-discrimination obligations to most areas of life and to embrace conduct by private (or non-state) actors in addition to the government. Landlords, restaurants, employers, transportation companies, water and electricity providers, parks, swimming pools, and insurance schemes ought to be prohibited from discriminating on any of the above-mentioned grounds. The second thing to notice is that the list is not closed. Other grounds of discrimination may be prohibited. So far little universal consensus has emerged, but the UN Committees responsible for monitoring legal obligations under the Covenants of 1966 have extended the non-discrimination obligation to prohibit discrimination with regard to the rights in those treaties on grounds of sexual orientation, health status (including HIV or AIDS), physical or mental disability, and nationality. The third point to understand is that in some cases, drawing a distinction between people on a particular ground may be justified as reasonable, for example religious schools may restrict employment to followers of the relevant faith.

A case concerning age discrimination provides a further example. An Australian airline pilot, Mr Love, complained to the UN Human Rights Committee that his compulsory retirement from Australian Airlines at the age of 60 constituted unlawful discrimination under the Covenant. First, the Committee determined that age could be considered as a prohibited ground of discrimination and considered that age was a prohibited 'status' even if not explicitly mentioned in the equality provisions of the Covenant. Second, it was noted that mandatory retirement ages may actually provide workers protection by limiting life-long working time. Third, the Human Rights Committee accepted that the distinction made on the basis of age pursued a legitimate aim: maximizing safety to passengers and others. This was neither arbitrary nor unreasonable. To paraphrase one of the members, Justice Bhagwati from the Indian Supreme Court: not every differentiation incurs the vice of discrimination.

Human rights reasoning also lies at the heart of new demands for equal rights in new areas such as same-sex marriage. Even before any developments could be discerned in international human rights law, the South African Constitutional Court found in favour of two women who wanted to get married to each other. At one level, the case turns on the application of the Constitution; at another level, the decision is a logical extension of the philosophy of human rights. Writing for the whole Court, Justice Albie Sachs explained:

> A democratic, universalistic, caring and aspirationally egalitarian society embraces everyone and accepts people for who they are.

To penalise people for being who and what they are is profoundly disrespectful of the human personality and violatory of equality. Equality means equal concern and respect across difference. It does not presuppose the elimination or suppression of difference. Respect for human rights requires the affirmation of self, not the denial of self. Equality therefore does not imply a levelling or homogenisation of behaviour or extolling one form as supreme, and another as inferior, but an acknowledgement and acceptance of difference. At the very least, it affirms that difference should not be the basis for exclusion, marginalisation and stigma. At best, it celebrates the vitality that difference brings to any society.

A major equality issue concerns the restrictions that are permitted with regard to non-nationals. At one level, discrimination against non-nationals is a form of racism or xenophobia which is offensive and irrational. At another level, it is accepted that states can control immigration, can limit who can vote and stand in elections, and may limit access to employment or aspects of health care or education. Nevertheless, human rights principles demand that any such distinctions are justified as proportionate to a legitimate aim. So a rule that precludes foreigners from obtaining employment with the secret services could be considered proportionate to the aims of ensuring national security. Rules that demand higher university fees from foreigners could be proportionate to the aim of ensuring access to education for the local tax-paying population. On the other hand, migrant workers are not only protected by a specialized Convention (in force for only a few states), but also through a number of international opinions and interpretative statements. The UN Committee on the Elimination of Racial Discrimination recently stated that:

> while States parties may refuse to offer jobs to non-citizens without a work permit, all individuals are entitled to the enjoyment of

labour and employment rights, including the freedom of assembly and association, once an employment relationship has been initiated until it is terminated.

The same Committee reminds these states to:

Take effective measures to prevent and redress the serious problems commonly faced by non-citizen workers, in particular by non-citizen domestic workers, including debt bondage, passport retention, illegal confinement, rape and physical assault.

This brings us to the phenomenon of human trafficking.

Trafficking illustrates how the human rights framework is moving away from a simple focus on equality to develop new protections. Trafficking exposes its victims to further abuses in the country of destination, including violations of the right not to be subjected to forced labour and the right to be protected from inhumane treatment. In 2000, a new treaty was adopted to 'Prevent, Suppress and Punish Trafficking in Persons'. The treaty addresses traffickers who use deception or coercion in their recruitment, transportation, transfer, harbouring, or receipt of persons. Their purpose is exploitation, which is stated to include 'at a minimum, the exploitation of the prostitution of others or other forms of sexual exploitation, forced labour or services, slavery or practices similar to slavery, servitude or the removal of organs'. The treaty states that the consent of the victim is irrelevant. Rather than address the victims of trafficking, the treaty focuses on creating criminal jurisdiction over the traffickers. The fate of the trafficked women, however, is left to rather vague demands that the receiving country consider adopting measures to allow the women to remain. States remain ready to use the option of deportation of the trafficked women, thus discouraging these women from seeking protection, and in some cases exposing them to further risks in their country of origin. The promise of human rights for all men and women is largely failing the victims of trafficking. The principle of equality is proving to be rather empty when considered against the rule that allows for non-nationals to be deported.

One problem with the human right not to be discriminated against is that it usually assumes that you are being discriminated against in the enjoyment of your other rights. Migrant workers and the victims of trafficking do not possess a right to enter a country or to have access to the employment market. Furthermore, discrimination principles rely on the idea of a comparator. Human rights are violated when you are treated less favourably than someone else in a comparable position. What if there is no obvious comparator? Women who are discriminated against for being pregnant, or minorities whose culture risks extinction, may find that discrimination principles are of little use. A further problem relates to affirmative action (also known as positive discrimination). Human rights principles do allow for positive discrimination in the context of racial and sex discrimination, but such measures clearly run the risk of being challenged as fresh forms of discrimination. The acceptability of any affirmative action programme will depend entirely on the context. Again, different societies will have different priorities

> **Box 35: Amnesty International, *It's in Our Hands: Stop Violence against Women* (2004)***
>
> One of the achievements of women's rights activists has been to demonstrate that violence against women is a human rights violation. This changes the perception of violence against women from a private matter to one of public concern and means that public authorities are required to take action.

The parallel development of international and regional human rights standards reinforces this accountability. Framing violence against women as a human rights issue creates a common language for the work of anti-violence activists and facilitates global and regional networks ... The human rights framework also specifies governments' obligations under international law to promote and protect women's human rights. It provides mechanisms for holding governments to account if they fail to meet these obligations.

One of the most powerful features of the human rights framework is the core principle that human rights are universal – all people have equal rights by virtue of being human. The appeal to universality counters one of the most common excuses used to justify violence against women, that it is acceptable because it is part of the society's culture. All human rights should be enjoyed by all people, and culture or tradition do not excuse the violation of women's basic human rights. Universality does not impose uniformity or deny diversity. Human rights can be universal only if understood in terms of the rich range of different cultures and experiences.

with regard to achieving the representation of certain minorities or disadvantaged groups in various sectors of society.

Despite these fundamental difficulties with the concept of non-discrimination, the human rights framework and the notion of equality have been adapted to create a powerful campaign to deal with violence against women (see Box 35). There has been a shift away from issues of formal equality and actions by the state towards highlighting state inaction and private responsibilities (see Box 36).

15. Amnesty International's high-profile campaign, supported here by Patrick Stewart, encourages people to speak out against domestic violence as a human rights issue

The purpose of our campaign is not to portray women as victims and stigmatize men as perpetrators; it is to condemn the act of violence itself. That will require all of us to change, not only as organizations and institutions but as individuals.

This campaign is like no other that we have organized before because it calls on each of us to take responsibility. Violence against women will only end when each one of us is ready to make that pledge: not to do it, or permit others to do it, or tolerate it, or rest until it is eradicated.

Chapter 9
The death penalty

This final chapter on the death penalty serves as a reminder of how our attitudes with regard to what constitutes a human rights question change over time. For the drafters of the 18th-century French and American Declarations, it was inconceivable that abolition of the death penalty could form part of their proclamations of rights. Even in 1945, there was no agreement on this issue among the united nations that had fought the Second World War, and the 1948 Universal Declaration is silent on this point. In modern times, about half of the states in the world have formally abolished the death penalty, and actual use of the death penalty by the remainder is concentrated in a rather small number of states (see Box 37).

Some would question whether the death penalty should really be seen as a human rights issue. If treaties that outlaw the death penalty remain unsigned, and elected legislators choose to keep this form of punishment, then the grounds for saying that it is universally prohibited are thin. The simple response to these arguments is that the death penalty violates the right to life and is therefore wrong, and that furthermore, if we are convinced that torture and inhuman punishment is absolutely prohibited then the ultimate irrevocable punishment of execution should also be prohibited. For some organizations and for many individuals, there is no need to go beyond such logical conclusions.

Box 37: Amnesty International, *Facts and Figures on the Death Penalty* (2006)*

In 2005, 94 per cent of all known executions took place in China, Iran, Saudi Arabia and the USA. Based on public reports available, Amnesty International estimated that at least 1,770 people were executed in China during the year, although the true figures were believed to be much higher. A Chinese legal expert was quoted as stating the figure for executions is approximately 8,000 based on information from local officials and judges, but official national statistics on the application of the death penalty remained classified as a state secret.

Iran executed at least 94 people and Saudi Arabia at least 86, but the totals may have been much higher. Sixty people were executed in the USA.

Executions have been carried out by the following methods since 2000:

Beheading – (in Saudi Arabia, Iraq)

Electrocution – (in USA)

Hanging – (in Egypt, Iran, Japan, Jordan, Pakistan, Singapore and other countries)

Lethal injection – (in China, Guatemala, Philippines, Thailand, USA)

Shooting – (in Belarus, China, Somalia, Taiwan, Uzbekistan, Viet Nam and other countries)

Stoning – (in Afghanistan, Iran)

Executions are known to have been carried out in the following countries in 2005:*

Bangladesh, Belarus, China, Indonesia, Iran, Iraq, Japan, Jordan, Korea (North), Kuwait, Libya, Mongolia, Pakistan,

Palestinian Authority, Saudi Arabia, Singapore, Somalia, Taiwan, USA, Uzbekistan, Viet Nam, Yemen

Death sentences are known to have been imposed in the following countries and territories in 2005:

Afghanistan, Algeria, Bahamas, Bahrain, Bangladesh, Belize, Barbados, Burkina Faso, Burundi, China, Congo (Democratic Republic), Egypt, Ethiopia, Ghana, Guinea, India, Indonesia, Iran, Iraq, Jamaica, Japan, Jordan, Kazakstan, Korea (North), Korea (South), Kuwait, Laos, Lebanon, Libya, Malawi, Malaysia, Mali, Mongolia, Morocco, Nigeria, Oman, Pakistan, Philippines, Qatar, Saudi Arabia, Singapore, Somalia, Sri Lanka, Sudan, Syria, Taiwan, Tanzania, Trinidad And Tobago, United States of America, Uzbekistan, Viet Nam, Yemen, Zimbabwe

Nevertheless, as stated above, governments after the Second World War were in no mood to abolish the death penalty in their human rights instruments protecting the right to life. The major human rights treaties were drafted with built-in exceptions to the right to life; life could be taken by the state in the context of a judicially administered death penalty following a fair trial. Let us see how the human rights treaties which allow for the death penalty have been interpreted to include procedural safeguards, limits on which crimes may be punished with a death sentence, and on who may be executed, as well as prohibitions on certain forms of execution.

The notion of a prohibition on *arbitrary* deprivation of life means that a death sentence may only be imposed following a fair trial with appropriate safeguards, including a fair hearing by an independent and impartial tribunal, the presumption of innocence, minimum guarantees for the defence, and review by a higher tribunal.

There is agreement among states that imposition of the death penalty be limited to the most serious crimes: namely, intentional crimes with lethal or other extremely grave consequences. Increasingly, there are arguments about what sort of crime 'deserves' the death penalty, and this in turn can stimulate discussion about proportionality between offence and sentence. Although the death penalty is abolished in the European Union member states, the EU sees the abolition of the death penalty in other states as part of the 'progressive development of human rights'. In this regard, the EU considers that, where the death penalty has not been abolished, it should not be imposed for 'non-violent financial crimes or for non-violent religious practice or expression of conscience'.

Turning to the death penalty itself, we encounter the frontiers of what is, and what is not, accepted as a universal human right. Governments are divided about what is acceptable and what is not. But again, the idea that states, nations, peoples, or cultures are immutable is wrongheaded. South Africa abolished the death penalty as a result of its Constitutional Court's determination in 1995 that the death penalty violated the constitutional prohibition on cruel, inhuman, or degrading treatment. Other jurisdictions are continuing to assess when the death penalty may be unacceptable under their constitutional protections. The US Supreme Court held in 2002 that imposition of the death penalty on the 'mentally retarded' is prohibited as violating the constitutional prohibition on 'cruel and unusual punishments'. In 2005, the US Supreme Court held that it was unconstitutional for the death penalty to be imposed on those who were minors at the time of the offence. It is now therefore relatively uncontroversial that international norms prohibit the execution of juvenile offenders, the insane, and pregnant women.

The conditions surrounding execution have also given rise to an interesting set of prohibitions on *carrying out* the death penalty. First, the prohibition of the death penalty in some states (notably in Europe) has been interpreted to prevent those states extraditing or deporting individuals to face the death penalty elsewhere. Second, the anxiety of waiting for years to exhaust appeals is considered to amount to inhuman treatment (ironically, the solution is therefore to speed up the process between trial and execution). Third, the method of execution (such as the cyanide gas chamber used in California) could be found to constitute cruel and inhuman treatment.

At the end of this chapter, we highlight the extent to which the movement against the death penalty has led to developments in various aspects of human rights law. The determination to find ways of preventing executions, in the absence of an absolute universal ban on the death penalty in international human rights law, has resulted in interpretations of the notion of 'inhuman and degrading treatment' to encompass the method of execution, the time spent on death row, conditions of incarceration, the uncertainty of the appeals process, and the unfairness of the trial. Prohibition of the death penalty has been extended to prevent abolitionist states from deporting or extraditing to a state where the individual would be subject to a possible death penalty; the rules for fair trial have constantly been re-examined to ensure proper access to documentation and qualified counsel, and attempts have been made to consider more carefully allegations of discrimination in the justice system. Greater attention to mental illness would, one would hope, be one further development; however, there remains evidence that, even though the US Constitutional ban on execution of the 'mentally retarded' represents a universal norm, some jurisdictions will simply redefine what constitutes 'mentally retarded' and continue to execute those deemed to fall on the wrong side of the new line.

So, insisting that the death penalty is a human rights issue has served to highlight serious problems with regard to

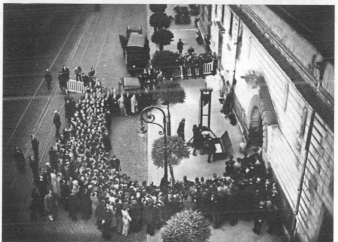

16. A lethal injection chamber in the US today, and the last public execution in France, which took place in 1937 in Versailles by guillotine. The guillotine was introduced in France as a humane method of execution in 1792 and was used until 1977

representation, due process, discrimination, and prison conditions. Nevertheless, universal abolition of the death penalty remains a long way off. With scientific advances concerning DNA testing and other methods of identification, there is greater confidence that only the guilty are being executed. This diminishes the force of the argument that the death penalty remains unacceptable due to the risk of executing an innocent human being. Arguments concerning the cruelty of the death penalty can be met with new 'humane' ways to inflict death. Ultimately, human rights principles ask us to see that the death penalty is an unnecessary interference with the right to life as no immediate threat to another life is posed by the condemned human being.

Final remarks

The content of human rights is no longer solely determined through appeals to reason and natural law. Human rights texts have been negotiated and adopted at the national and international levels. These texts have a certain moral force based on the context of their adoption. Authoritarianism, deprivation, and slaughter are counterpoised with the promise of a future based on human rights.

But the promise of human rights remains unfulfilled around the world. Daily reports of violent abuse, injustice, and the denial of basic subsistence rights leave no room to doubt that we live in a world of human rights violations. Human rights reporting exposes the worst cases but remains frustrated in the face of governments' failure to live up to their promise that they will step in to protect populations from genocide, war crimes, ethnic cleansing, and crimes against humanity. Human rights foreign policies stop far short of effective action in such crisis situations. The failure to prevent genocides in the 20th century is fading from memory.

At another level, we have discussed the ways in which human rights bodies have developed human rights principles related to torture, the right to life, detention, freedom of expression, privacy, food, education, health, housing, work, and equality. Many topics have admittedly been skated over or left out. One aim of this book was to give the reader insights into how human rights need to be considered separately to appreciate the complexity of their implementation in any one situation. The language and logic of human rights should be seen as routes to arguing about claims and countervailing interests; human rights are not a closed book, but rather part of an ongoing conversation.

For human rights to have a greater impact, they have to appeal to people's imaginations and become properly part of their vocabulary. For human rights really to take hold, they will have to be understood and fully internalized. This means continuing to debate and develop the principles of human rights so that they meet people's needs and expectations, refined and adapted to their local contexts. The vocabulary of human rights can help to formulate these demands. Expressing conflicts in terms of human rights language can reveal the competing interests at stake and suggest the appropriate procedures for resolving the tension.

Human rights risk being seen, however, as alien, imposed, and instrumental for other ends unless more work is done to conquer the limited meaning they are often given. Those who insist on a narrow meaning seek to confine human rights to an historically based determination of specific governmental duties to refrain from infringing traditional liberties; the wider vision of human rights allows for consideration of the problems of hunger, poverty, and violence facing billions of people (see Box 38).

Even where the human rights movement has sought to expand the horizons of human rights protection, as with the campaign against violence against women, this may again be seen as imperfect. Some critics argue that human rights organizations may tend to generate a narrative that reinforces images of helpless victims oppressed by an alien culture; in turn, this could be said to continue imperialism by other means. These critics argue that the biggest challenge is to understand the origins of such inequality and violence, rather than simply categorizing violence against women as a question of human rights (see Box 39). Human rights campaigners are learning that insisting on respect for human rights is not the only way to change the world. But insisting on human rights can be instrumental to ensuring that a wider variety of voices and suggestions are heard.

It is remarkable that an oft-heard plea is that human rights should be less 'politicized'. This makes no sense. Human rights *are* political: they articulate the relationship between individuals and groups within a community and their relationship with others, particularly those with power and authority. That's national politics. If states set up a Human Rights Council at the UN, where governments discuss each other's records, that's international politics. The hope that governments will somehow set aside

> **Box 39: Ratna Kapur, *Erotic Justice: Law and the New Politics of Postcolonialism***
>
> The class, cultural, religious and racial differences between women are collapsed under the category of gender through women's common experience of sexual violence and objectification by men. Differences between women are simply understood as cultural, without exploring or elaborating on how the cultural context was shaped and influenced in and through the colonial encounter – an encounter between the West and 'the Rest'. To miss this part of the argument is to present a narrative of women's exploitation and subordination that does not implicate the ways in which race, religion and imperial ambition constituted the vortex of knowledge that affords us a historically grounded and contextualized understanding of that experience.

their economic and foreign policy interests to arrive at objective 'apolitical' assessments of the human rights behaviour of other states is vain indeed.

Individuals and groups will continue to feel empowered by the language of human rights and by the framework that has grown up to develop solidarity in ensuring respect for these rights. When these claims are articulated as human rights demands, this often represents political participation rather than isolated individualism. The point here is to change things, including how human rights themselves are conceived. We have seen throughout this book that the protection of human rights is a dynamic process based on developing demands and changing views about what human rights require. The human rights movement is now concerned with global social justice. Human rights are vibrant not static.

We might finish by returning to the ways in which the expression 'human rights' has featured in literature. In his 1910 novel *Howards End*, E. M. Forster used the term 'human rights' to highlight the injustice of the way the unmarried pregnant Helen Schlegel is being treated by society, and the feelings of solidarity that the other heroine, Margaret, feels towards her sister Helen.

> Margaret's anger and terror increased every moment. How dare these men label her sister! What horrors lay ahead! What impertinences that shelter under the name of science! The pack was turning on Helen, to deny her human rights, and it seemed to Margaret that all Schlegels were threatened with her.

The passage illustrates how, then as now, human rights claims result simply from a sense of injustice and a feeling of solidarity.

References

* indicates that the text is available on the companion website for this Very Short Introduction http://hei.unige.ch/human-rights-vsi

Chapter 1

Review of the Implementation of the Human Rights Act, July 2006*

W. A. Edmundson, *An Introduction to Rights* (Cambridge: Cambridge University Press, 2004), p. 191

R. Falk, 'Rights', in *The Oxford Companion to Politics of the World*, 2nd edn, ed. J. Krieger (Oxford: Oxford University Press, 2001), pp. 734–5

Magna Carta (1215)*

English Bill of Rights (1689)*

J. Locke, *The Second Treatise of Government*, 1690 (New York: Macmillan, 1986), paras 6–8, 13, 221–2

J.-J. Rousseau, *The Social Contract, or Principles of Political Right*, anon. tr. 1791 (New York: Hafner, 1947), chs VII and VIII

T. Paine, *Rights of Man*, 1791 (Harmondsworth: Penguin, 1969), at 228, 69, 70*

E. Burke, *Reflections on the Revolution in France*, ed. L. G. Mitchell (Oxford: Oxford University Press, 1993)

A. Gerwith, 'Are There Any Absolute Rights?', in *Theories of Rights*, ed. J. Waldron (Oxford: Oxford University Press, 1984), pp. 91–109, at 108

J. Bentham, *Anarchical Fallacies; being an examination of the Declaration of Rights issued during the French Revolution*, Vol. 2,

The Works of Jeremy Bentham, ed. J. Bowring (Edinburgh: William Tait, 1843)*

A. Sen, *Development as Freedom* (New York: Knopf, 1999), pp. 228–9

S. Howe, *Empire: A Very Short Introduction* (Oxford: Oxford University Press, 2002), p. 3

R. Rorty, 'Human Rights, Rationality, and Sentimentality', in *On Human Rights: The Oxford Amnesty Lectures*, ed. S. Shute and S. Hurley (Oxford: Oxford University Press, 1993), pp. 111–34, at 118–19, 122

M. Kundera, *Immortality* (London: Faber and Faber, 1991), pp. 150–4

M. Glendon, *Rights Talk: The Impoverishment of Political Discourse* (New York: The Free Press, 1991), pp. 16, 45–6

Chapter 2

H. Lauterpacht, *An International Bill of the Rights of Man* (New York: Columbia University Press, 1945)

P. Alston, 'Conjuring Up New Human Rights: A Proposal for Quality Control', *American Journal of International Law,* Vol. 78 (1984): 607–21

B. A. W. Simpson, *Human Rights and the End of Empire: Britain and the Genesis of the European Convention* (Oxford: Oxford University Press, 2004); and P. French, *Younghusband The Last Great Imperial Adventurer* (London: Harper Perennial, 2004), p. 296

Final Act of the Havana Meeting of the American Institute of International Law, *American Journal of International Law,* Vol. 11, No. 2, Supplement: Official Documents (April 1917) , pp. 47–53

W. Wilson, 'Fourteen Points Speech', delivered in Joint Session, 8 January 1918*

Covenant of League of Nations (1924)*

A. Cassese, *Human Rights in a Changing World* (Cambridge: Polity Press, 1990), pp. 17–18

EarthRights International, 'Final Settlement Reached in Doe v. Unocal', 21 March 2005* (I have discussed some legal aspects of the litigation in my *Human Rights Obligations of Non-State Actors* (Oxford: Oxford University Press, 2006) at 252–70, 443–50.)

P. G. Lauren, *The Evolution of International Human Rights: Visions Seen* (Philadelphia: University of Pennsylvania Press, 1998), p. 135

L. Sohn, 'How American International Lawyers Prepared for the San Francisco Bill of Rights', *American Journal of International Law,* 89 (1995): 540, 543 (for details on Lapradelle)

Déclaration des droits internationaux de l'homme, Resolution of the
   Institute of International Law (1927)*

H. G. Wells, *The Rights of Man: or what are we fighting for?*
   (Harmondsworth: Penguin, 1940), pp. 8–9, 11, 12, 31, 52

J. Dilloway, *Human Rights and World Order: Two Discourses for the
   H. G. Wells Society* (H. G. Wells Society, 1998). The Declaration
   and Appendix to Wells's *Phoenix: A Summary of the Inescapable
   Conditions of World Reorganisation* (London: Secker and
   Warburg, 1942) are both reproduced in this publication.

F. D. Roosevelt, *State of the Union Address 1941* (known as the 'Four
   Freedoms Speech'), delivered 6 January 1941*

Trial of German Major War Criminals (Goering et al.), International
   Military Tribunal (Nuremberg) Judgement and Sentence, 30
   September and 1 October 1946 (London: HMSO, Cmd 6964), at
   40, 41 (chapter 'Law of the Charter')*

Joint Declaration of France, Great Britain and Russia, 24 May 1915*

2005 World Summit Outcome, 16 September 2005* (on the
   responsibility to protect)

Human Rights Watch World Report 2004, *Human Rights and Armed
   Conflict*

A. A. An-Na'im, 'Problems of Universal Cultural Legitimacy for
   Human Rights', in *Human Rights in Africa: Cross-Cultural
   Perspectives*, A. A. An-Na'im and F. M. Deng (eds) (Washington
   DC: Brookings Institute, 1990), pp. 331–67, at 350, 352

Evans v United Kingdom, Judgment of the European Court of Human
   Rights, 7 March 2006, at paras 46, 62, and 68*

Proclamation of Teheran, proclaimed by the International Conference
   on Human Rights at Teheran on 13 May 1968*

Chapter 3

The Responsibility to Protect: Report of the International
   Commission on Intervention and State Sovereignty
   (Ottowa: International Development Research Centre,
   2001)*

A. Clarke in *The Observer*, 6 December 1998, 'Words with Power to
   Stop Tyranny', p. 22

Ambassador Qiao Zonghauai, Statement to the UN Sub-Commission
   on the Promotion and Protection of Human Rights, 4 August 1999
   (NATO bombing)

President Yeltsin, OSCE Istanbul Summit, 18–19 November 1999

Y. Ghai, 'Rights, Duties and Responsibilities', in *Human Rights Solidarity*, AHRC Newsletter, 7(4) (1997), 9 at 10

A. Sen, *Development as Freedom* (New York: Knopf, 1999), pp. 246, 248

US Bureau of Democracy, Human Rights, and Labor, *Country Reports on Human Rights Practices 2005**

B. F. Lowenkron, Assistant Secretary of State, Testimony Before the House International Relations Subcommittee on Africa, Global Human Rights and International Operations, 16 March 2006*

Address by Secretary of State Madeleine K. Albright to the UN Human Rights Commission, Palais des Nations, 23 March 2000*

Right of Reply, by Chinese Ambassador Qiao Zonghuai to the UN Human Rights Commission, 23 March 2000

J. S. Nye, *Soft Power: The Means to Success in World Politics* (New York: Public Affairs, 2004), p. 55

EU Annual Report on Human Rights, 2005*

Vienna Declaration and Programme of Action, adopted by the World Conference on Human Rights in Vienna on 25 June 1993*

United Kingdom position on trade and labour standards is taken from *Eliminating World Poverty: Making Globalization Work for the Poor*, Cm 5006, December 2000, at p. 74

R. Cook, 'Making the Difference', speech given at the Amnesty Human Rights Festival, London, 16 October 1998

Swiss Human Rights Policy pamphlet, produced by the Federal Department of Foreign Affairs, Political Affairs Division IV, No. 42925/4

Human Rights Council established by General Assembly Resolution A/RES/60/251 of 15 March 2006*

C. Patten, *Not Quite the Diplomat: Home Truths about World Affairs* (London: Penguin Books, 2006), p. 194

Special Procedures of the Commission on Human Rights 2005 communications*

J. Kirkpatrick, 'UN Human Rights Panel Needs Some Entry Standards', *International Herald Tribune*, 14 May 2003*

Human Rights Watch, 'UN: Credibility at Stake for Rights Commission', 10 March 2004*

Statement of Mary Robinson, UN High Commissioner for Human Rights, on Situation in Chechnya, Russian Federation*

New York Times, 'In Tour of Africa, US Pulls its Punches on Human Rights', 15 December 1997, p. 10

Chapter 4

Convention Against Torture and Other Cruel, Inhuman or Degrading Treatment or Punishment, entered into force 26 June 1987*

J. S. Bybee, Assistant Attorney-General, *Memorandum for Alberto R. Gonzales, Counsel to the President, Re: Standards of Conduct for Interrogation under 18 U.S.C. §§2340–2340A*, 1 August 2002*

Body of Principles for the Protection of All Persons under Any Form of Detention or Imprisonment, G.A. res. 43/173, annex, 43 UN GAOR Supp. (No. 49) at 298, UN Doc. A/43/49 (1988)*

US Attorney-General Alberto Gonzales's comments on torture, as reported by BBC News in 'Top US Official Denies "torture"' on 7 March 2006*

Public Committee Against Torture in Israel and Others v State of Israel and Others, Israel Supreme Court, 6 September 1999*

S. Lukes, 'Liberal Democratic Torture', *British Journal of Political Science*, Vol. 36 (2005): 1–16, at 13

Hamdan v. Donald H. Rumsfeld, Secretary of Defense, et. al., 548 US – (2006)*

US Department of Defense, Military Commission Instruction, No. 10, 24 March 2006*

P. T. King, quoted in Carl Hulse, 'An Unexpected Collision over Detainees', *New York Times*, 15 September 2006*

'On Terrorists and Torturers' – Statement by UN High Commissioner for Human Rights, Louise Arbour, 7 December 2005*

Chapter 5

Basic Principles on the Use of Force and Firearms by Law Enforcement Officials, Adopted by the Eighth United Nations Congress on the Prevention of Crime and the Treatment of Offenders, Havana, Cuba, 27 August to 7 September 1990*

N. Mahfous, *Al-Ahram*, 2 March 1989

P. Benenson, 'The Forgotten Prisoners', *The Observer Weekend Review*, London, 28 May 1961, p. 21*

D. Kretzmer, 'Targeted Killing of Suspected Terrorists: Extra-Judicial Executions or Legitimate Means of Defence?', *European Journal of International Law*, Vol. 16 (2005): 171–212

Second Periodic Report of the United States to the UN Committee against Torture, p. 50*

Report of Five Independent Investigators of the United Nations
Commission of Human Rights on the Situation of Detainees at
Guantánamo Bay, 15 February 2006, UN Doc. E/CN.4/2006/120*

E. Posner, 'A Threat that Belongs Behind Bars', in *The New York Times*,
25 June 2006*

Chapter 6

De May v Roberts, 46 Mich. 160, 165, 9N.W. 146, 149 (1881)

L. Brandeis and S. Warren, 'The Right to Privacy', *Harvard Law
Review*, Vol. 4 (1890): 193

H. Charlesworth, C. Chinkin, and S. Wright, 'Feminist Approaches to
International Law', *American Journal of International Law*,
Vol. 85(4), (1991): 613–45

Hatton and Others v United Kingdom [2003] ECHR 338*

Chapter 7

The Economist, 'Righting Wrongs', 16 August 2001*

Kamayani Bali Mahabal, 'Enforcing the Right to Food in India – The
Impact of Social Activism', *ESR Review*, March 2004*

Soobramoney v Minister of Health, Republic of South Africa
Constitutional Court, Case CCT 32/97, 27 November 1997*

UN Committee on Economic, Social and Cultural Rights, *General
Comment 13 on the Right to Education*, 8 December 1999*

Annual Reports of the UN Special Rapporteur on the Right to
Education*

ILO C182: *Convention Concerning the Prohibition and Immediate
Action for the Elimination of the Worst Forms of Child Labour*,
1999*

Campbell and Cosans v The United Kingdom [1982] ECHR 1*

Committee on Economic, Social and Cultural Rights, *General
Comment 14 on the Right to the Highest Attainable Standard of
Health*, 11 August 2000*

Decision of the General Council of the WTO on Implementation of
paragraph 6 of the Doha Declaration on the TRIPS Agreement and
Public Health, WT/L/540 and Corr.1, 1 September 2003*

G8 Gleneagles Summit Document on Africa 2005*

S. Leckie, 'The Right to Housing', in *Economic, Social and Cultural
Rights: A Textbook*, 2nd edn, A. Eide, C. Krause, and A. Rosas (eds)
(The Hague: Nijhoff, 2001), pp. 149–68 at 150

Committee on Economic, Social and Cultural Rights, *General Comment No. 4 on the Right to Adequate Housing*, 13 December 1991*

Committee on Economic, Social and Cultural Rights, *General Comment No. 7 on the Right to Adequate Housing: Forced Evictions*, 20 May 1997*

OECD, Guidelines for Aid Agencies on Involuntary Displacement and Resettlement in Development Projects, Paris 1992*

World Bank Operational Policy 4.12: Involuntary Resettlement, December 2001*

Narmada Bachao Andolan v Union of India AIR (2000) SC 3751, at 3827*

ILO Declaration on Fundamental Principles and Rights at Work, 86th Session, Geneva, June 1998*

Committee on Economic, Social and Cultural Rights, *General Comment No. 18 on the Right to Work*, 6 February 2006*

Chapter 8

Human Rights Committee, *General Comment 18 on Non-Discrimination*, 10 November 1989*

Minister of Home Affairs v Fourie, South African Constitutional Court (2005) at para 60*

Committee on the Elimination of Racial Discrimination, *General Recommendation 30 on Discrimination against Non-Citizens*, 2004, para 35*

Protocol to Prevent, Suppress and Punish Trafficking in Persons, Especially Women and Children, supplementing the United Nations Convention against Transnational Organized Crime, 2000*

Chapter 9

Amnesty International, *Facts and Figures on the Death Penalty*, 1 January 2006*

Declaration by the Presidency on Behalf of the European Union to Mark the First World Day against the Death Penalty, 10 October 2003*

Council of the European Union, *Guidelines to EU Policy Towards Third Countries on the Death Penalty*, 3 June 1998, para III(i)*

The State v Makwanyane and Mchunu, Constitutional Court of the
  Republic of South Africa, Case No. CCT/3/94, 6 June 1995*
Atkins v Virginia 526 U.S. 304 (2002)*
Roper v Simmons 543 U.S. _ (2005)*
Soering v United Kingdom [1989] ECHR 14*

Final remarks

E. M. Forster, *Howards End*, 1910 (Harmondsworth: Penguin, 1989),
  p. 282

Boxes

1   O. Harvey and M. Lea, '35,000 Back Sun on Rights', *Online Sun*,
     accessed 9 August 2006;* 'Give Us Back Our Rights', *Sunday
     Telegraph*, 14 May 2006*
2   M. Wollstonecraft, 'Dedication to Monsieur Talleyrand-Périgord',
     in *A Vindication of the Rights of Woman: with strictures and
     political and moral subjects* (Boston: Thomas and Andrews,
     1792)*
3   K. Marx, *On the Jewish Question* (1843), excerpted in M. R.
     Ishay (ed.), *The Human Rights Reader: Major Political Essays,
     Speeches, and Documents from the Bible to the Present* (New York:
     Routledge, 1997), pp. 189–99 at 196*
4   M. Tushnet, 'An Essay on Rights', *Texas Law Review*, Vol. 62
     (1984): 1363–403 at 1394
5   H. G. Wells, *The Rights of Man: or what are we fighting for?*
     (Harmondsworth: Penguin, 1940), p. 52
6   W. A. Schabas, *Preventing Genocide and Mass Killing: The
     Challenge for the United Nations* (London: Minority Rights Group
     International, 2006), p. 8*
7   *Prosecutor v Radislav Krstic*, Case # IT-98-33-A, ICTY (Appeals
     Chamber), 19 April 2004*
8   Rome Statute of the International Criminal Court (1998)*
9   Mr Vyshinsky (USSR), UN General Assembly, 180th plenary
     meeting, 9 December 1948, summary records, at 855–6.
10 Mr Davies (UK), UN General Assembly, 181st plenary meeting,
     10 December 1948, summary records, at 884.
11 P. Sieghart, *The Lawful Rights of Mankind: An Introduction to
     the International Legal Code of Human Rights* (Oxford: Oxford
     University Press, 1986), p. vii

12 UK Foreign Secretary Robin Cook, Speech to Royal Institute of International Affairs, Chatham House, 28 January 2000, reproduced in *Human Rights: Foreign and Commonwealth Office Annual Report 2000*, Cm 4774, p. 135

13 US Department of State, *2005 Country Reports on Human Rights Practices*; Sudan*

14 Special Procedures of the UN Commission for Human Rights*

15 K. Roth, 'Despots Pretending to Spot and Shame Despots', 17 April 2001, *International Herald Tribune*

16 Opinion of Lord Hope of Craighead in *A and others v Secretary of State for the Home Department* [2005] UKHL 71, at para 103*

17 US Department of Justice, Memorandum for James B. Comey, Deputy Attorney General, 30 December 2004, p. 10*

18 F. Jessberger, 'Bad Torture – Good Torture? What International Criminal Lawyers May Learn from the Recent Trial of Police Officers in Germany', *Journal of International Criminal Justice*, Vol. 3 (2005): 1059–73

19 Opinion of Lord Rodger of Earlsferry, in *A and others [No. 2] v Secretary of State for the Home Department* [2005] UKHL 71, at para 132*

20 Human Rights Watch 2005, *Still at Risk: Diplomatic Assurances No Safeguard Against Torture*

21 *Agiza v Sweden*, Communication No. 233/2003, UN Doc. CAT/C/34/D/233/2003 (2005)*

22 *Rotura v Romania* [2000] ECHR 192, at paras 57–9*

23 R. Walmsley, *World Prison Population List*, 6th edn (London: International Centre for Prison Studies, Kings College London, 2005)

24 US Department of State, *2005 Country Reports on Human Rights:* Russia*

25 Princess Caroline – Federal Constitutional Court of Germany, 1 BvR 653/96, 15 December 1999, at para 60*

26 *von Hannover v Germany* [2004] ECHR 294, at paras 76–7*

27 *The Economist*, 'Righting Wrongs', 16 August 2001*

28 J. Shultz, 'Bringing It All Back Home', *New Internationalist*, 342 (2002): 34–5, at 34

29 *Christian Education South Africa v Minister of Education*, Constitutional Court of South Africa, 18 August 2000, at para 15*

30 Convention on the Rights of the Child (1989), Article 29*

31 Report of the Special Rapporteur on the Right of Everyone to the Enjoyment of the Highest Attainable Standard of Physical and Mental Health, Paul Hunt, paras 40–2*

32 UN General Assembly 2005, Summit Outcome, para 68(i)*

33 UN Conference on Human Settlements (Habitat Agenda) 1996, para 60*

34 N. Klein, *No Logo* (London: Flamingo, 2001), pp. 210–11

35 Amnesty International, *It's in Our Hands: Stop Violence against Women*, 2004, AI Index: ACT 77/001/2004 at 11–12*

36 I. Khan, Amnesty International, *It's in Our Hands: Stop Violence against Women*, 2004, AI Index: ACT 77/001/2004, at v*

37 Amnesty International, *Facts and Figures on the Death Penalty*, 2006*, *Death Sentences and Executions 2005*

38 M. Mutua, *Human Rights: A Political and Cultural Critique* (Philadelphia: University of Pennsylvania Press, 2002), p. 14; C. Douzinas, *The End of Human Rights: Critical Legal Thought at the Turn of the Century* (Oxford: Hart Publishing, 2000), p. 12

39 R. Kapur, *Erotic Justice: Law and the New Politics of Postcolonialism* (London: Glasshouse Press, 2005), p. 104

Further reading

The companion website for this Very Short Introduction can be found at http://hei.unige.ch/human-rights-vsi. On this website, you will find links to some of the texts we have mentioned, as well as a useful set of links to human rights sites.

The books listed below offer particular insights into the world of human rights; most of them are short introductions. Readers who want to follow up a specific topic may find it useful to start with *The Essentials of Human Rights*, edited by Rhona Smith and Christien van den Anker (London: Hodder Arnold, 2005). Arranged in an **A-Z format**, it contains over 150 short entries covering religious values, theory, the institutional framework, legal instruments, the actual rights and freedoms, monitoring, international humanitarian and criminal law, the reality of human rights violations in the different regions, and the future of human rights. Each entry contains references for further reading. Those wanting a more legal approach can find summaries and analyses of **human rights cases** across a wide range of Commonwealth and international jurisdictions in Nihal Jayawickrama's *The Judicial Application of Human Rights Law: National, Regional and International Jurisprudence* (Cambridge: Cambridge University Press, 2002). For readers looking for detail on the application of **human rights law in the United Kingdom**, a good reference is *The Law of Human Rights*, by Richard Clayton and Hugh Tomlinson, 2nd edn. (Oxford: Oxford University Press, 2007).

Ways of looking at human rights

A good place to start to look at the place of human rights in modern **moral and political philosophy** is *On Human Rights*, edited by Stephen Shute and Susan Hurley (New York: Basic Books, 1993). This includes entries by: Steven Lukes, John Rawls, Catherine MacKinnon, Richard Rorty, Jean-François Lyotard, Agnes Heller, and Jon Elster. For a light-hearted look at some of the problems encountered in the search for a utopian system, see Steven Lukes's *The Curious Enlightenment of Professor Caritat: A Comedy of Ideas* (London: Verso, 1996).

For a **historico-sociological** look at how *rights* transmuted into *human rights*, see Anthony Woodiwiss, *Human Rights* (London: Routledge, 2005). He suggests we see rights as the products of power (rights to property and contract) being transformed in the 1940s into international human rights which can now be used in practical ways to protect people, not only from oppressive regimes, but also to fashion greater equality for 'the global majority' by encroaching on the same right to property which foretells the advent of human rights.

For a new look at the **philosophical** dimension of human rights seen against concerns about the 'war on terror', see Conor Gearty's Hamlyn Lectures: *Can Human Rights Survive?* (Cambridge: Cambridge University Press, 2006). Gearty's perspective is informed by his insight that there is a danger of us becoming alienated from human rights activism through the judicial reification of rights.

For an examination of the **historical context** in which the idea of human rights emerged, see Micheline Ishay's *The History of Human Rights: From Ancient Times to the Globalization Era* (Berkeley: University of California Press, 2004). Ishay uses history to shed light on what she calls 'misconceptions' regarding human rights. She argues that religion contains humanistic elements that anticipated the modern conception of human rights and highlights the positive contribution of religion to the evolution of human rights. She also traces the precursors to rights thinking through different religious and other texts, including the Hammurabi Code from Babylon, the Hebrew Bible, the New Testament, and the Koran, and looks at Confucianism, Hinduism, and Buddhism. Ishay brings out the contribution of socialist ideas which developed against the background of 19th-century industrialization. The book covers arguments about the supposed antagonism between human rights and security and finishes with reflections on the impact of globalization on human rights. A useful companion is Ishay's *The Human Rights Reader: Major Political Essays, Speeches, and Documents from the Bible to the Present* (New York: Routledge, 1997).

For a perspective that suggests that the legal approach has been over-emphasized and asks us to consider the different ways in which the other social sciences understand human rights, see Michael Freeman, *Human Rights: An Interdisciplinary Approach* (Cambridge: Polity Press, 2002). This book asks some hard questions about the universality of human rights and the structures that give rise to human rights violations.

For an account of the international human rights regime and its deficiencies in addressing the demands of people for social justice in an era of **globalization and market pressures**, see Koen De Feyter, *Human Rights: Social Justice in the Age of the Market* (London: Zed Books, 2005). The **shortfalls of human rights thinking** and the human rights movement in the face of globalization are discussed from a critical perspective by Upendra Baxi in his *The Future of Human Rights* (New Delhi: Oxford University Press, 2002).

For an enthusiastic historical overview of **the people and ideas** that have contributed to the human rights movement and the development of international human rights law, see Paul Lauren, *The Evolution of International Human Rights: Visions Seen*, 2nd edn (Philadelphia: University of Pennsylvania Press, 2003).

Human rights protection

Samantha Power's award-winning book recounts how the concept of **genocide** was invented by Raphael Lemkin and how politicians in the United States have failed to act in the face of genocide in the 20th century: *'A Problem from Hell': America and the Age of Genocide* (New York: Harper Collins, 2003). Power's book goes to the heart of the question of US foreign policy and asks bigger questions. In her words: 'We have all been bystanders to genocide. The crucial question is why.'

For an account of the drafting of the **Universal Declaration of Human Rights** from the inside, see John Humphrey, *Human Rights and the United Nations: A Great Adventure* (Dobbs Ferry: Transnational, 1984), pp. 1–77.

For a collection of short essays which attempt to look at different aspects of human rights protection from the **victim's perspective**, see *The Universal Declaration of Human Rights: Fifty Years and Beyond*, edited by Yael Danieli, Elsa Stamatopoulou, and Clarence Dias (New York: Baywood, 1999).

Human Rights, Human Wrongs (Oxford: Oxford University Press, 2003), edited by Nicholas Owen, contains stimulating essays on the ethics of **military intervention** and a number of contemporary debates on how to tackle **crimes against humanity** in today's world.

Tim Allen's *Trial Justice: The International Criminal Court and the Lord's Resistance Army* (London: Zed Books, 2006) provides a detailed overview of some of the crimes committed in Uganda and examines the problems facing the Court in the context of the arrest warrants issued in 2005.

For a recent set of contributions on the role of **civil society**, see Paul Gready (ed.) *Fighting for Human Rights* (London: Routledge, 2004). And for detailed examples of which sorts of international discussion have been most **effective** in securing change, see Thomas Risse,

Stephen Ropp, and Kathryn Sikkink (eds), *The Power of Human Rights: International Norms and Domestic Change* (Cambridge: Cambridge University Press, 1999).

Julie Mertus, *The United Nations and Human Rights: A Guide for a New Era* (London: Routledge, 2005) is an introduction to the **multiple UN bodies** that deal with human rights and contains excerpts from UN reports to give a flavour of the UN's approach.

For an interdisciplinary look at the question of the **universality** of human rights from an 'area studies' perspective, see David Forsythe and Patrice McMahon (eds), *Human Rights and Diversity: Area Studies Revisited* (Lincoln: University of Nebraska Press, 2003). These essays show how geographical regions and cultures relate to human rights practice. Examples include an examination of child labour in South Asia, female genital mutilation in Africa, and women's rights in Muslim states. The book asks sophisticated questions about how to engage in a cross-cultural dialogue about human rights and to admit that universality cannot be taken as a given (and that one may have to acknowledge the limits of taking a human rights approach in some circumstances).

Foreign policy and international relations

For a riveting account of the struggle to get the **United Nations** to react to the **torture and disappearances** in Latin America, see Iain Guest's *Behind the Disappearances: Argentina's Dirty War Against Human Rights and the United Nations* (Philadelphia: University of Pennsylvania Press, 1990).

Aryeh Neihr's story of his founding of **Human Rights Watch** explains from an insider's perspective how the organization works to hold the 'United States accountable for abuses by governments of other countries because of U.S. support': *Taking Liberties: Four Decades in the Struggle for Rights* (New York: Public Affairs, 2003).

For a view of **US human rights foreign policy** from the inside by the former Assistant Secretary of State for Democracy, Human Rights and Labour, John Shattuck, see *Freedom on Fire: Human Rights Wars and America's Response* (Cambridge, Mass.: Harvard University Press, 2003).

A more sceptical exposure of the way human rights are invoked in **British and US foreign policy** can be found in Kirsten Sellars's book, *The Rise and Rise of Human Rights* (Phoenix Hill: Sutton Publishing, 2002).

A helpful introduction to human rights in **international relations** from a political science perspective is David Forsythe's *Human Rights in International Relations*, 2nd edn (Cambridge: Cambridge University Press, 2006).

For an examination of the Western governments' **pattern of condemnations** and sanctions in response to human rights violations in other countries, see the empirical study by Katerina Tomaševski, *Responding to Human Rights Violations 1946–1999* (The Hague: Martinus Nijhoff, 2000).

Particular topics covered in this Very Short Introduction

For an accessible set of essays by activists and scholars on the contemporary challenges of **torture**, see Kenneth Roth and Minky Worden (eds), *Torture: Does It Make Us Safer? Is It Ever OK?* (New York: The New Press, 2005).

The legitimacy and legality of the US and UK **detention** of 'enemy combatants' and 'suspected terrorists' is examined by Philippe Sands in his widely read book *Lawless World: The Making and Breaking of Global Rules*, updated version (London: Allen Lane, 2006). The book also looks at the torture issue and contains a critical examination of the British legal justification for the 2003 Iraq war.

Joshua Rozenberg's book, *Privacy and the Press* (Oxford: Oxford University Press, 2004) looks at the tension between **privacy** and the media under UK law from the perspective of a journalist. The key principles are illustrated through his engaging discussion of English cases.

For expert analysis of how rights to **health** and **housing** are implemented by courts in jurisdictions such as India, South Africa, and Canada, see *The Role of Judges in Implementing Economic, Social and Cultural Rights*, edited by Yash Ghai and Jill Cottrell (London: Interights, 2004).

For the sociology of the way the **concept of race** has been used and the way anti-racism has developed at the national and international level into a human rights framework, see Michael Banton, *The International Politics of Race* (Cambridge: Polity Press, 2002).

Women and Human Rights by the late Katerina Tomaševski (London: Zed Books, 1995) outlines some of the successes and failures in using human rights to achieve women's human rights. Written as an action manual to bring **women's rights** into the development process, the book also provides the reader with an introduction to the key issues.

Sex Rights, edited by Nicholas Bamforth (Oxford: Oxford University Press, 2005), is a collection of essays developing human rights arguments for greater **equality** and **autonomy** for those discriminated against on grounds of **sex or sexual orientation**. The links between violence and those who are perceived as a threat to traditional gender roles are discussed and alternative strategies are proposed for engaging with opposition based on religion or culture.

Further discussion regarding the rights discussed in this introduction can be found in an **A-Z format** in the *International Human Rights Lexicon* by Susan Marks and Andrew Clapham (Oxford: Oxford University Press, 2005). At one level, this introduction picks up some of the themes developed more fully in the following *Lexicon* entries:

death penalty, detention, development, disability, disappearances, education, fair trial, food, globalization, health, housing, international crimes, media, privacy, protest, racism, religion, sexuality, terrorism, torture, universality, women, and work.

Some dramatic works that take human rights violations as their starting point include the plays *The Jail Diary of Albie Sachs* (1981) by David Edgar, and *Death and the Maiden* (1991) by Ariel Dorfman; we might also mention the recent film *Hotel Rwanda* (2004) directed by Terry George.

Annex: The Universal Declaration of Human Rights

Preamble

Whereas recognition of the inherent dignity and of the equal and inalienable rights of all members of the human family is the foundation of freedom, justice and peace in the world,

Whereas disregard and contempt for human rights have resulted in barbarous acts which have outraged the conscience of mankind, and the advent of a world in which human beings shall enjoy freedom of speech and belief and freedom from fear and want has been proclaimed as the highest aspiration of the common people,

Whereas it is essential, if man is not to be compelled to have recourse, as a last resort, to rebellion against tyranny and oppression, that human rights should be protected by the rule of law,

Whereas it is essential to promote the development of friendly relations between nations,

Whereas the peoples of the United Nations have in the Charter reaffirmed their faith in fundamental human rights, in the dignity and worth of the human person and in the equal rights of men and women and have determined to promote social progress and better standards of life in larger freedom,

Whereas Member States have pledged themselves to achieve, in cooperation with the United Nations, the promotion of

universal respect for and observance of human rights and
fundamental freedoms,

Whereas a common understanding of these rights and freedoms is of
the greatest importance for the full realization of this pledge,

Now, therefore,

The General Assembly,

Proclaims this Universal Declaration of Human Rights as a common
standard of achievement for all peoples and all nations, to the end that
every individual and every organ of society, keeping this Declaration
constantly in mind, shall strive by teaching and education to promote
respect for these rights and freedoms and by progressive measures,
national and international, to secure their universal and effective
recognition and observance, both among the peoples of Member
States themselves and among the peoples of territories under their
jurisdiction.

Article 1

All human beings are born free and equal in dignity and rights. They
are endowed with reason and conscience and should act towards one
another in a spirit of brotherhood.

Article 2

Everyone is entitled to all the rights and freedoms set forth in this
Declaration, without distinction of any kind, such as race, colour, sex,
language, religion, political or other opinion, national or social origin,
property, birth or other status.

Furthermore, no distinction shall be made on the basis of the political,
jurisdictional or international status of the country or territory to
which a person belongs, whether it be independent, trust,
non-self-governing or under any other limitation of sovereignty.

Article 3

Everyone has the right to life, liberty and security of person.

Article 4

No one shall be held in slavery or servitude; slavery and the slave trade shall be prohibited in all their forms.

Article 5

No one shall be subjected to torture or to cruel, inhuman or degrading treatment or punishment.

Article 6

Everyone has the right to recognition everywhere as a person before the law.

Article 7

All are equal before the law and are entitled without any discrimination to equal protection of the law. All are entitled to equal protection against any discrimination in violation of this Declaration and against any incitement to such discrimination.

Article 8

Everyone has the right to an effective remedy by the competent national tribunals for acts violating the fundamental rights granted him by the constitution or by law.

Article 9

No one shall be subjected to arbitrary arrest, detention or exile.

Article 10

Everyone is entitled in full equality to a fair and public hearing by an independent and impartial tribunal, in the determinationof his rights and obligations and of any criminal charge against him.

Article 11

1. Everyone charged with a penal offence has the right to be presumed innocent until proved guilty according to law in a

public trial at which he has had all the guarantees necessary for his defence.

2. No one shall be held guilty of any penal offence on account of any act or omission which did not constitute a penal offence, under national or international law, at the time when it was committed. Nor shall a heavier penalty be imposed than the one that was applicable at the time the penal offence was committed.

Article 12

No one shall be subjected to arbitrary interference with his privacy, family, home or correspondence, nor to attacks upon his honour and reputation. Everyone has the right to the protection of the law against such interference or attacks.

Article 13

1. Everyone has the right to freedom of movement and residence within the borders of each State.
2. Everyone has the right to leave any country, including his own, and to return to his country.

Article 14

1. Everyone has the right to seek and to enjoy in other countries asylum from persecution.

2. This right may not be invoked in the case of prosecutions genuinely arising from non-political crimes or from acts contrary to the purposes and principles of the United Nations.

Article 15

1. Everyone has the right to a nationality.
2. No one shall be arbitrarily deprived of his nationality nor denied the right to change his nationality.

Article 16

1. Men and women of full age, without any limitation due to race, nationality or religion, have the right to marry and to found a family. They are entitled to equal rights as to marriage, during marriage and at its dissolution.

2. Marriage shall be entered into only with the free and full consent of the intending spouses.

3. The family is the natural and fundamental group unit of society and is entitled to protection by society and the State.

Article 17

1. Everyone has the right to own property alone as well as in association with others.

2. No one shall be arbitrarily deprived of his property.

Article 18

Everyone has the right to freedom of thought, conscience and religion; this right includes freedom to change his religion or belief, and freedom, either alone or in community with others and in public or private, to manifest his religion or belief in teaching, practice, worship and observance.

Article 19

Everyone has the right to freedom of opinion and expression; this right includes freedom to hold opinions without interference and to seek, receive and impart information and ideas through any media and regardless of frontiers.

Article 20

1. Everyone has the right to freedom of peaceful assembly and association.

2. No one may be compelled to belong to an association.

Article 21

1. Everyone has the right to take part in the government of his country, directly or through freely chosen representatives.

2. Everyone has the right to equal access to public service in his country.

3. The will of the people shall be the basis of the authority of government; this will shall be expressed in periodic and genuine elections which shall be by universal and equal suffrage and shall be held by secret vote or by equivalent free voting procedures.

Article 22

Everyone, as a member of society, has the right to social security and is entitled to realization, through national effort and international co-operation and in accordance with the organization and resources of each State, of the economic, social and cultural rights indispensable for his dignity and the free development of his personality.

Article 23

1. Everyone has the right to work, to free choice of employment, to just and favourable conditions of work and to protection against unemployment.

2. Everyone, without any discrimination, has the right to equal pay for equal work.

3. Everyone who works has the right to just and favourable remuneration ensuring for himself and his family an existence worthy of human dignity, and supplemented, if necessary, by other means of social protection.

4. Everyone has the right to form and to join trade unions for the protection of his interests.

Article 24

Everyone has the right to rest and leisure, including reasonable limitation of working hours and periodic holidays with pay.

Article 25

1. Everyone has the right to a standard of living adequate for the health and well-being of himself and of his family, including food, clothing, housing and medical care and necessary social services, and the right to security in the event of unemployment, sickness, disability, widowhood, old age or other lack of livelihood in circumstances beyond his control.

2. Motherhood and childhood are entitled to special care and assistance. All children, whether born in or out of wedlock, shall enjoy the same social protection.

Article 26

1. Everyone has the right to education. Education shall be free, at least in the elementary and fundamental stages. Elementary education shall be compulsory. Technical and professional education shall be made generally available and higher education shall be equally accessible to all on the basis of merit.

2. Education shall be directed to the full development of the human personality and to the strengthening of respect for human rights and fundamental freedoms. It shall promote understanding, tolerance and friendship among all nations, racial or religious groups, and shall further the activities of the United Nations for the maintenance of peace.

3. Parents have a prior right to choose the kind of education that shall be given to their children.

Article 27

1. Everyone has the right freely to participate in the cultural life of the community, to enjoy the arts and to share in scientific advancement and its benefits.

2. Everyone has the right to the protection of the moral and material interests resulting from any scientific, literary or artistic production of which he is the author.

Article 28

Everyone is entitled to a social and international order in which the rights and freedoms set forth in this Declaration can be fully realized.

Article 29

1. Everyone has duties to the community in which alone the free and full development of his personality is possible.

2. In the exercise of his rights and freedoms, everyone shall be subject only to such limitations as are determined by law solely for the purpose of securing due recognition and respect for the rights and freedoms of others and of meeting the just requirements of morality, public order and the general welfare in a democratic society.

3. These rights and freedoms may in no case be exercised contrary to the purposes and principles of the United Nations.

Article 30

Nothing in this Declaration may be interpreted as implying for any State, group or person any right to engage in any activity or to perform any act aimed at the destruction of any of the rights and freedoms set forth herein.

Index

Index

Expand your collection of
VERY SHORT INTRODUCTIONS

THE FRENCH REVOLUTION

A Very Short Introduction

William Doyle

Beginning with a discussion of familiar images of the French Revolution, garnered from Dickens, Baroness Orczy, and Tolstoy, this short introduction leads the reader to the realization that we are still living with the legacy of the French Revolution. It destroyed age-old cultural, institutional, and social structures in France and beyond. William Doyle shows how the *ancien régime* became *ancien* as well as examining cases in which achievement failed to match ambition, exploring its consequences in the arenas of public affairs and responsible government, and ending with thoughts on why the revolution has been so controversial.

'A brilliant combination of narrative and analysis, this masterly essay provides the best introduction to its subject in any language.'

Tim Blanning, University of Cambridge

www.oup.co.uk/isbn/0-19-285396-1

ROUSSEAU
A Very Short Introduction
Robert Wokler

Rousseau was both a central figure of the European Enlightenment and its most formidable critic. In this study of his life, works, sources, and influence, Robert Wokler shows how Rousseau's account of the trappings of civilization across a wide range of disciplines was inspired by ideals of humanity's self-realization in a condition of unfettered freedom.

> 'Remarkably well-informed . . . this at once chronological and thematic treatment of Rousseau's thought makes plain its unity and coherence. Addressing both philosophical and political sources as well as influences, the work includes a fine bibliographical commentary . . . and commends itself through the clarity of its exposition and the rigour of its analysis.'
>
> **Raymond Trousson, *Dix-huitieme siecle***

> 'One of the best-informed, most balanced, short general introductions to Rousseau . . . in English. . . . Wokler's study leaves a vivid impression of Rousseau's uniqueness and originality as a thinker.'
>
> **Graeme Garrard, *History of Political Thought***

www.oup.co.uk/isbn/0-19-280198-8

MARX
A Very Short Introduction
Peter Singer

Peter Singer has succeeded in identifying the central vision that unifies Marx's thought. He thus makes it possible, in remarkably few pages, for us to grasp Marx's views as a whole, rather than as an economist or a social scientist. He explains alienation, historical materialism, the economic theory of Capital and Marx's ideas of communism in plain English, and concludes with an assessment of Marx's legacy.

> 'An admirably balanced portrait of the man and his achievement.'
>
> **Philip Toynbee, *Observer***

www.oup.co.uk/isbn/0-19-285405-4

ANIMAL RIGHTS
A Very Short Introduction
David DeGrazia

Do animals have moral rights? If so, what does this mean?
What sorts of mental lives do animals have, and how
should we understand their welfare? After putting forward
answers to these questions, David DeGrazia explores the
implications for how we treat animals in connection with
our diet, zoos, and research.

'This is an ideal introduction to the topic. David DeGrazia
does a superb job of bringing all the key issues together
in a balanced way, in a volume that is both short and very
readable.'

Peter Singer, Princeton University

'Historically aware, philosophically sensitive, and with
many well-chosen examples, this book would be hard to
beat as a philosophical introduction to animal rights.'

Roger Crisp, Oxford University

www.oup.co.uk/isbn/0-19-285360-0